Official Cambridge Exam Preparation

B2
FIRST
FOR SCHOOLS 5

WITHOUT ANSWERS

AUTHENTIC PRACTICE TESTS

 WITH AUDIO

Shaftesbury Road, Cambridge CB2 8EA, United Kingdom

One Liberty Plaza, 20th Floor, New York, NY 10006, USA

477 Williamstown Road, Port Melbourne, VIC 3207, Australia

314–321, 3rd Floor, Plot 3, Splendor Forum, Jasola District Centre, New Delhi – 110025, India

103 Penang Road, #05–06/07, Visioncrest Commercial, Singapore 238467

Cambridge University Press & Assessment is a department of the University of Cambridge.

We share the University's mission to contribute to society through the pursuit of education, learning and research at the highest international levels of excellence.

www.cambridge.org
Information on this title: www.cambridge.org/9781009273022

© Cambridge University Press & Assessment 2023

This publication is in copyright. Subject to statutory exception and to the provisions of relevant collective licensing agreements, no reproduction of any part may take place without the written permission of Cambridge University Press & Assessment.

First published 2023

20 19 18 17 16 15 14 13 12 11 10 9 8 7 6 5 4

Printed in Great Britain by Ashford Colour Limited

A catalogue record for this publication is available from the British Library

ISBN 978-1-009-27302-2 Student's Book without Answers with Audio

Cambridge University Press & Assessment has no responsibility for the persistence or accuracy of URLs for external or third-party internet websites referred to in this publication and does not guarantee that any content on such websites is, or will remain, accurate or appropriate. Information regarding prices, travel timetables, and other factual information given in this work is correct at the time of first printing but Cambridge University Press & Assessment does not guarantee the accuracy of such information thereafter.

Contents

Introduction

Prepare for the exam with practice tests from Cambridge

Inside you'll find four authentic examination papers from Cambridge University Press & Assessment. They are the perfect way to practise – EXACTLY like the real exam.

Why are they unique?

All our authentic practice tests go through the same design process as the B2 First for Schools exam. We check every single part of our practice tests with real students under exam conditions, to make sure we give you the most authentic experience possible.

Students can practise these tests on their own or with the help of a teacher to familiarise themselves with the exam format, understand the scoring system and practise exam technique.

Cambridge English Qualifications	CEFR Level	UK National Qualifications
C2 Proficiency	C2	3
C1 Advanced	C1	2
B2 First for Schools	B2	1
B1 Preliminary for Schools	B1	Entry 3
A2 Key for Schools	A2	Entry 2

Further information

The information contained in this practice book is designed to be an overview of the exam. For a full description of all of the above exams, including information about task types, testing focus and preparation, please see the relevant handbooks, which can be obtained from the Cambridge English website at: **cambridgeenglish.org**.

The structure of *B2 First for Schools*: an overview

The *Cambridge English Qualifications B2 First for Schools* examination consists of four papers:

Reading and Use of English: 1 hour 15 minutes
Candidates need to be able to understand texts from publications such as fiction and non-fiction books, journals, newspapers and magazines.

Writing: 1 hour 20 minutes
Candidates have to show that they can produce two different pieces of writing: a compulsory essay in Part 1 and one from a choice of four tasks in Part 2. Question 5 in Part 2 is based on a set reading text. These practice tests do not include this task as the set text changes every two years. You can find more information about the set text at the Cambridge English website (see page 4 for details).

Listening: 40 minutes approximately
Candidates need to show they can understand the meaning of a range of spoken material, including lectures, radio broadcasts, speeches and talks.

Speaking: 14 minutes (or 20 minutes for groups of 3)
Candidates take the Speaking test with another candidate or in a group of three, and are tested on their ability to take part in different types of interaction: with the examiner, with the other candidate and by themselves.

	Overall length	Number of tasks/parts	Number of items
Reading and Use of English	1 hour and 15 minutes	7	52
Writing	1 hour and 20 minutes	2	-
Listening	approx. 40 mins	4	30
Speaking	14 mins	4	-
Total	3 hours and 29 mins approximately		

Grading

All candidates receive a Statement of Results and candidates whose performance ranges between CEFR Levels B1 and C1 (Cambridge English Scale scores of 140–190) also receive a certificate.

- Candidates who achieve **Grade A** (Cambridge English Scale scores of 180–190) receive the B2 First Certificate in English stating that they demonstrated ability at Level C1.

- Candidates who achieve **Grade B** or **C** (Cambridge English Scale scores of 160–179) receive the B2 First Certificate in English at Level B2.

- Candidates whose performance is below B2 level, but falls within **Level B1** (Cambridge English Scale scores of 140–159), receive a Cambridge English certificate stating that they have demonstrated ability at Level B1.

For further information on grading and results, go to the website (see page 4 for details).

Speaking: an overview for candidates

You take the Speaking test with another candidate (possibly two candidates), referred to here as your partner. There are two examiners. One will speak to you and your partner and the other will be listening. Both examiners will award marks.

Part 1 (2 minutes)

The examiner asks you and your partner questions about yourselves. You may be asked about things like 'your home town', 'your interests', 'your career plans', etc.

Part 2 (4 minutes)

The examiner gives you two photographs and asks you to talk about them for one minute. The examiner then asks your partner a question about your photographs and your partner responds briefly.

Then the examiner gives your partner two different photographs. Your partner talks about these photographs for one minute. This time the examiner asks you a question about your partner's photographs and you respond briefly.

Part 3 (4 minutes)

The examiner asks you and your partner to talk together for two minutes. They give you a task to look at so you can think about and discuss an idea, giving reasons for your opinion. For example, you may be asked to think about some changes in the world, or about spending free time with your family.

After you have discussed the task for about two minutes with your partner, the examiner will ask you a follow-up question, which you should discuss for a further minute.

Part 4 (4 minutes)

The examiner asks some further questions related to your topic from Part 3. You may comment on your partner's answers if you wish.

Test 1

READING AND USE OF ENGLISH (1 hour 15 minutes)

Part 1

For questions **1–8**, read the text below and decide which answer (**A**, **B**, **C** or **D**) best fits each gap. There is an example at the beginning **(0)**.

Mark your answers on the separate answer sheet.

Example:

0 **A** keeps   **B** gets   **C** carries   **D** goes

0	A	B	C	D
	●	o	o	o

The world's deepest underwater cave?

Polish explorer Krzysztof Starnawski **(0)** .... returning to Hranická Propast, an underwater cave in the Czech Republic. His fascination with the cave began during his first dive there, when he started to **(1)** .... that it might be possible to go far deeper than any other dive had ever taken him before.

Returning a few years later, Starnawski dived to 200 m, but was stopped by a narrow passage in the rock that **(2)** .... to a tunnel. He lowered a probe – a weight on the end of a long rope – and still didn't hit the bottom of the cave.

On his next visit, the following year, he found that the passage had widened **(3)** .... He swam through it down to 265 m. Then Starnawski went back again, **(4)** .... by a remotely-operated underwater robot, which **(5)** .... its way to a record-breaking depth of 404 m.

Starnawski is **(6)** .... to continue to explore this mysterious, **(7)** .... unending cave, believing that it may **(8)** .... out to be even deeper!

1 **A** suspect   **B** wonder   **C** expect   **D** assess

2 **A** guided   **B** led   **C** headed   **D** ran

3 **A** largely   **B** entirely   **C** excessively   **D** considerably

4 **A** attended   **B** provided   **C** accompanied   **D** supplied

5 **A** broke   **B** made   **C** went   **D** gave

6 **A** committed   **B** determined   **C** intended   **D** dedicated

7 **A** apparently   **B** distinctly   **C** noticeably   **D** particularly

8 **A** set   **B** end   **C** turn   **D** come

Part 2

For questions **9–16**, read the text below and think of the word which best fits each gap. Use only **one** word in each gap. There is an example at the beginning **(0)**.

Write your answers **IN CAPITAL LETTERS on the separate answer sheet**.

Example: | **0** | A | L | L | | | | | | | | | | | | | | | | |

Plastic roads

The amount of plastic waste produced around the world is growing **(0)** .... the time. But one man sees this as an opportunity rather than a problem. Dr Rajagopalan Vasudevan, a professor of chemistry from the Indian city of Madurai has **(9)** .... up with a way to re-use plastic waste, as **(10)** .... as improving road quality. His method, **(11)** .... he first developed in 2001, requires hardly **(12)** .... changes to existing road-laying techniques.

The method involves breaking plastic **(13)** .... small pieces, then combining them **(14)** .... the traditional road-building components in order to produce a strong, long-lasting material. All kinds of plastic can be used, even plastic that is normally considered **(15)** .... costly to be worth recycling.

There are now over 5,000 km of Dr Vasudevan's plastic roads in use in rural India. He travels throughout the country instructing engineers on exactly **(16)** .... to build roads in this way. His philosophy is: we create the waste, so it is up to us to find an effective solution.

Part 3

For questions **17–24**, read the text below. Use the word given in capitals at the end of some of the lines to form a word that fits in the gap **in the same line**. There is an example at the beginning **(0)**.

Write your answers **IN CAPITAL LETTERS on the separate answer sheet.**

Example: | 0 | S | U | I | T | A | B | L | E | | | | | | | | |

Is chess a sport?

Should chess be considered a sport, **(0)** .... to be included   **SUIT**

in events like the Olympic games? In my view, there's no doubt about

it. The point of sport is to test people's physical ability. So, I'm not

(17) .... chess as a game and I have great respect for players   **CRITIC**

who take part in chess **(18)** .... I'm just saying it's not a sport.   **CHAMPION**

There are certainly other sports which don't require athletes to be

(19) .... – target shooting is one. But there's a significant   **ENERGY**

difference between shooting and playing chess. In chess, the physical actions

themselves are not what the **(20)** .... are trying to be good at.   **COMPETE**

Instead, chess makes enormous **(21)** .... demands   **INTELLECT**

on players. Just look at the skill displayed by the grandmasters.

So, my **(22)** .... to describe chess as a sport does not   **WILLING**

affect my **(23)** .... for it. Chess calls for extreme mental   **ADMIRE**

(24) .... and is a very enjoyable activity.   **STRONG**

Part 4

For questions **25–30**, complete the second sentence so that it has a similar meaning to the first sentence, using the word given. **Do not change the word given**. You must use between **two** and **five** words, including the word given. Here is an example **(0)**.

Example:

0   Prizes are given out when the school year finishes.

PLACE

Prize-giving ……………………………………………………… end of the school year.

The gap can be filled by the words 'takes place at the', so you write:

Example:	**0**	*TAKES PLACE AT THE*

Write **only** the missing words **IN CAPITAL LETTERS on the separate answer sheet**.

---

25   I bought these dance shoes two weeks ago and I've only just started to feel comfortable in them.

USED

It's taken me two weeks ………………………………………………… wearing these dance shoes.

26   That boy's sister won an Olympic medal!

WHOSE

That's ………………………………………………… won an Olympic medal!

27   Can you look after my bag for me for a moment?

EYE

Can you ………………………………………………… my bag for me for a moment?

28 The teacher advised us against bringing too much money with us on our school trip.

NOT

The teacher's advice .... too much money with us on our school trip.

29 Let's go straight to the main stage when we get to the festival.

SOON

Let's go to the main stage .... at the festival.

30 I really don't mind which day we have the party on.

CONCERNED

As .... , we can have the party on any day at all.

Part 5

You are going to read an article about a successful British songwriter and music producer called Jamie Scott. For questions **31–36**, choose the answer (**A**, **B**, **C** or **D**) which you think fits best according to the text.

Mark your answers on the separate answer sheet.

A career in music

Reporter Eamonn Forde met UK songwriter and music producer Jamie Scott.

Jamie Scott has written and produced some of the biggest hits in the UK music business. He says his mother was 'an amazing singer' who also got him interested in the guitar. The only radio he heard in his house was a local radio station for middle-aged people, which goes some way to explaining what influenced him as he was growing up. He says he was 12 before he heard a contemporary song. At about the same time, he had to choose between tennis, which he played at national level, and music – he was spending his lunchtimes in the music room at school working out songs on the piano. 'With the tennis playing, I was at quite a high level,' he says. 'But it was not what I wanted to do for the rest of my life. It was just too much hard work.'

At 17, he left school to try to make it as a performer. He was part of a duo with a friend who, while not sharing his enthusiasm for making a career out of performing, was a reasonably accomplished guitarist. 'I went to my parents and I just broke down,' he recalls. 'I told them this is what I wanted to do, that I had been writing lyrics in economics lessons and I had been playing the piano every day when everyone else was out playing.' His dad was understanding and gave him 18 months to try and make it; but if he didn't, he would have to get a job. After a few near misses with record labels, he was signed to a music publisher when he was 19, off the back of one song. However, record labels were only interested in him as a solo act and so he had to split with his friend.

In the end, it was behind the scenes rather than on stage where he would make his name. After a difficult period signed to a record label in the UK, he asked them to let him go and he switched to another label

to release a new album. Fame and fortune did not follow. 'It feels like to me in my own artist career that I've been in the wrong place at the wrong time for most of that time,' he says. 'But as a writer I've been in the right place at the right time.'

Writing for others is where he was to find his feet. 'I'd like to think that I am one of the main writers in the UK that UK labels look to send up-and-coming artists to,' he says. This, he believes, helps launch their careers.

Sometimes he has to explain to the artists he's helping that writing with an eye on the charts – writing something that's likely to sell well – is nothing to be ashamed of. 'Why? Why don't you want to? Don't you want 10 million people streaming your music next month? I'm not saying that they should write a bad song, but we should get to something that they think is amazing and that I think is amazing.'

It is refreshing in an age of false modesty in the world of pop music to hear someone speak so bluntly about wanting to write huge songs that go to number one. There is no sense of arrogance or entitlement with Scott; he just realised long ago that he wants to write number ones and that he has a natural ability to do it. So, rather than tie himself in knots trying to make himself sound acceptable to other people, he just gets on with it.

'That's the endgame for when I go into the studio with someone,' he says. 'Whatever happens, we need to state that this is on the global level and that we *line 64* need to write the best music of next year. It's not just about what's cool. We want to write classic modern pop songs.'

31   What do we learn about Jamie Scott's childhood in the first paragraph?

  A   It was clear to him that he would work in the music industry.
  B   He wished he had had access to more musical instruments at home.
  C   He regretted having to give up the idea of playing sport professionally.
  D   The music of a previous generation was an inspiration to him.

32   What is emphasised about Scott in the second paragraph?

  A   how determined he was
  B   how little support he had
  C   how quickly his talent was recognised
  D   how much better a musician he was than his friend

33   What does Scott suggest in the third paragraph?

  A   It was his decision to become a songwriter.
  B   It is more difficult to become a performer than a songwriter.
  C   Bad luck prevented him from becoming a successful performer.
  D   He was unprepared for the challenges he faced as a performer and songwriter.

34   What opinion does Scott express in the fifth paragraph?

  A   Few writers are able to write a song that will appeal to large numbers of people.
  B   Only a song that has had a great deal of work put into it can succeed.
  C   Unless he likes a song himself other people are unlikely to buy it.
  D   Just because a song is popular does not mean it lacks quality.

35   What is the reporter's attitude towards Scott in the sixth paragraph?

  A   He appreciates the quality of his song-writing.
  B   He respects his commitment to his work.
  C   He admires him for his honesty.
  D   He approves of his ambition.

36   What does 'this' refer to in line 64?

  A   the place where they are recording
  B   the work they are doing
  C   the style of their music
  D   the plan they have for the future

Part 6

You are going to read an article about a new world map. Six sentences have been removed from the article. Choose from the sentences **A–G** the one which fits each gap (**37–42**). There is one extra sentence which you do not need to use.

Mark your answers on the separate answer sheet.

A new map of the world

The decision to present the 2016 Good Design Award, one of Japan's most famous design honours, to Hajime Narukawa, the maker of the AuthaGraph World Map, came as a surprise to many. Given that previous winners have tended to be inventors of exciting new gadgets, people wondered what had impressed the judges about the design of a map.

The world map with which most of us are familiar uses what is known as the Mercator projection, a mapping technique developed in 1569 by map maker Gerardus Mercator. Though it is excellent for navigation, it significantly changes the size and proportion of areas of land and oceans. So while North America and Africa appear to be equal in size, in reality North America could fit inside Africa with plenty of room to spare. Similarly, though Brazil is more than five times larger than Alaska, it appears considerably smaller than it really is. **37** It is a task that is surprisingly hard to do accurately.

Over the years, there have been numerous attempts to deal with the issue. The Gall-Peters projection, for example, reduces the size of the regions near the poles. **38** This is because certain places appear oddly stretched. A similar change to the shapes of the continents occurs in the Mollweide projection, which attempts to show them more accurately by bending the lines of longitude. The Boggs eumorphic projection shows the correct shapes and sizes of everything on the map by cutting the globe into sections, but doing this means that vital information such as the distance between continents is not so clear, making the map impractical for navigation.

The AuthaGraph World Map appears to have solved these issues through the use of geometrical shapes. **39** These are then transferred onto the surface of what's called a tetrahedron, which is really just a four-sided pyramid. The tetrahedron can then be unfolded to form a flat rectangle. Doing this creates a two-dimensional map, which closely resembles the surface of the original globe.

The result is a world map unlike any other in its accuracy. **40** This makes Africa appear to be tilted on its side. Also the longitude and latitude lines are similarly distorted. Although these differences make the map look strangely unfamiliar, this is the closest anyone has ever come to capturing clearly and accurately the size and proportions of the Earth's surface.

In their announcement declaring the AuthaGraph World Map the overall winner, the officials at Good Design Award said it was selected because it 'faithfully represents all oceans and continents, including the neglected Antarctica,' and provides 'an advanced, precise perspective of our planet.' **41** This would involve some tricky mathematical calculations, but might well be something for map designers to consider.

While the AuthaGraph World Map is not ideal for navigation, it does have some practical applications, like helping us better understand how aeroplane flight paths are affected by the way the Earth's surface is curved. The map is also well suited to classroom use and has already been incorporated into Japanese textbooks. **42** Meanwhile, those eager to observe the world more accurately can purchase the map directly from the creator's website.

A Narukawa's concept first divides the globe into ninety-six equal triangles.

B This explains why such a strange-looking map is actually the most proportionate depiction of our planet ever seen.

C While this makes it easier to appreciate the relative size of continents and oceans, it doesn't completely solve the problem.

D Whether it will be adopted more widely than this remains to be seen.

E The continents curve upwards towards the edges of the map instead of going straight across it.

F The reason for differences like this has to do with the challenge of transforming a three-dimensional globe into a two-dimensional flat map.

G There was, however, a suggestion that the accuracy could be increased further in the future by cutting the world into even smaller chunks.

Part 7

You are going to read a magazine article about some young ballet dancers. For questions **43–52**, choose from the people (**A–D**). The people may be chosen more than once.

Mark your answers on the separate answer sheet.

___

Which person

says that they get their inspiration from different sources?	43
is irritated by the inaccurate ideas people have about ballet dancers?	44
says that the sacrifices they made were worth it?	45
describes how they felt about a change that was forced on them?	46
explains how ballet involves combining several actions simultaneously?	47
says that they have changed their attitude to criticism?	48
believes that their attitude to training makes them untypical?	49
describes how they were put off ballet by seeing the talent of others?	50
says that it took a while for them to demonstrate their potential?	51
says that they have found a way of dealing with their feelings prior to going on stage?	52

Young ballet dancers

A Maria Duncan

I was four when I reluctantly attended my first ballet class. I didn't take to it initially and there was little sign that I'd ever develop a genuine passion for it. I eventually began to show some promise, but my parents weren't happy with the dance school, and invested time and energy into finding a new one. I didn't see what the fuss was about because I got on well with my teacher and I was disappointed when the new one turned out to be much stricter. For ballet dancers, the reality is that artistic perfection can never be achieved. This used to frustrate me, but I've learnt to respond more positively to negative comments I get. Even people who've never tried ballet know how tough it is. From an early age, my mother instilled in me the importance of discipline and I appreciate that now, because I wouldn't have developed it independently.

B Leon Robson

It's hard to imagine something that makes more demands on your muscles and joints than ballet. Ask anyone who's attended a few classes as a hobby. They'll be aching afterwards in places they didn't know existed – and that includes fitness fanatics! There are lots of rather silly misconceptions about ballet dancers, and I think some things are exaggerated by the media. For a start, we don't all live in isolation, only mixing with other dancers. Anyway, the highlight of any dancer's life is taking part in a performance. I used to get very nervous beforehand, though, to the point where I could barely perform, but I've since learnt a few strategies I can apply, to good effect. And after a show, I take ages to unwind. I'm still buzzing and I tend to relive the excitement of the experience. I don't dwell on my errors too much, though.

C Melanie Haig

I started young, as most ballet dancers do, and seemed to show an aptitude for it more or less immediately. I remember being taken by my teacher to visit a professional ballet school and being intimidated by how good the girls were there, almost to the point of giving up. I sometimes think that the appeal of ballet to audiences is that they understand there's no way to achieve elegance and beauty without exceptional discipline, training and even physical pain. Ballet is challenging because a dancer is doing a number of things at any given moment to create something that seems effortless. Some of these, like lifting the stomach up while tensing leg muscles and relaxing the neck, can feel unnatural, and others, like standing on your toes, can even cause injury if repeated time and time again – as they inevitably are.

D Peter Moreno

While most people, including even the best ballet dancers, might think the routine of having to train for several hours every day is tough, I find it strangely reassuring and comforting rather than boring or restrictive. And it's not as if training ends when I leave the ballet school. At home I find myself doing basic exercises even while I'm watching TV or brushing my teeth. Ballet dominates your whole life – that was certainly my experience. I don't regret missing out on doing sport and not going to parties, though – I'm a far better dancer as a result. I've got loads of videos of top ballet dancers performing, some of them from many years ago and others more contemporary. I don't have a particular role model I'm obsessed with or think stands out for me. I pick up ideas from a range of dancers and styles.

WRITING (1 hour 20 minutes)

Part 1

You **must** answer this question. Write your answer in **140–190** words in an appropriate style on the separate answer sheet.

1   In your English class you have been talking about who makes the decisions at school. Now your English teacher has asked you to write an essay for homework.

Write your essay using **all** the notes and giving reasons for your point of view.

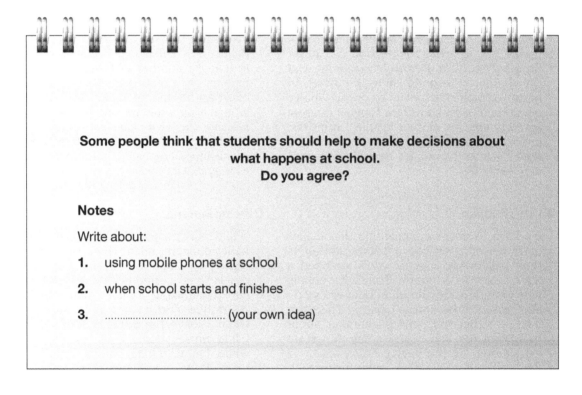

**Some people think that students should help to make decisions about what happens at school.
Do you agree?**

Notes

Write about:

1.   using mobile phones at school

2.   when school starts and finishes

3.   .... (your own idea)

Part 2

Write an answer to **one** of the questions **2–4** in this part. Write your answer in **140–190** words in an appropriate style on the separate answer sheet. Put the question number in the box at the top of the answer sheet.

---

2   You receive this email from your English friend, Emily. Write an email to Emily, answering her questions.

> Guess what! I've decided to learn your language, so we don't always have to speak in English. What will I find easy about learning your language? And what will be difficult for me? Should I learn with a teacher or do you think I can learn by myself? Any advice?
>
> Thanks
>
> Emily

Write your **email**.

3   You see this advert in an English language magazine for teenagers.

> *Articles wanted*
>
> ### Free time
>
> Tell us what the phrase 'free time' means to you. Do you prefer to be busy or just to relax in your leisure time?
>
> The best article will be published in the magazine.

Write your **article**.

4   You have seen this notice in an international magazine for teenagers.

> ### Stories wanted
>
> We are looking for stories for our new English-language magazine for teenagers. Your story must **begin** with this sentence:
>
> *It was Tom's first deep-sea diving lesson and he was quite nervous.*
>
> Your story must include:
> * a shark
> * a photograph

Write your **story**.

LISTENING (approximately 40 minutes)

Part 1

You will hear people talking in eight different situations.
For questions **1–8**, choose the best answer (**A**, **B** or **C**).

Listening test audio

1   You hear a boy talking about a visit to an art gallery.

    How did he feel about the visit?

    A put off by the amount of information available

    B pleased he was able to explore independently

    C confident that he would benefit from it

2   You hear a woman talking about taking part in a physical challenge for a television
    programme.

    Why does she mention the weather?

    A to illustrate their inadequate preparation

    B to describe how unpleasant the conditions were

    C to explain why the trip took longer than planned

3   You hear two students talking about a biology lesson they have just had about feeling dizzy.

    What do they both think about the lesson?

    A Other students spoiled it by laughing.

    B The teacher's use of video was very helpful.

    C It was difficult to grasp all the information.

4   You hear a girl talking about a novel she has just read.

    What is her opinion of it?

    A Some of the descriptions of places are irrelevant.

    B Reading it requires considerable concentration.

    C It underestimates the reader's intelligence.

5 You hear two friends discussing a television programme about an expedition in the Antarctic.

What do they agree about the programme?

A It provided too little advice about dealing with extreme cold.

B It gave too much scientific information.

C It took too long to introduce the people.

6 You hear a teenager talking about his trip to the theatre.

In telling the story, he shows that

A planning ahead can help to avoid disappointment.

B new experiences can produce unexpected results.

C putting someone else's happiness first is always a good idea.

7 You hear the introduction to a programme about a girl called Maria who is very good at computing.

Why did Maria's mother encourage her daughter to learn computer programming?

A She realised Maria had a natural talent for it.

B She wanted Maria to spend her time in a useful way.

C She knew it would be a good career for Maria.

8 You hear a boy telling a friend about a student exchange trip he went on.

What is the boy explaining?

A what to consider before going on the trip

B what was interesting about going on the trip

C what made him decide to go on the trip

Part 2

You will hear a woman called Anita Farrant talking about her work as a conservationist, protecting wildlife. For questions **9–18**, complete the sentences with a word or short phrase.

Listening test audio

Wildlife conservationist

Anita's family moved to **(9)** .... when she was still very young.

As a child, Anita enjoyed looking for **(10)** .... by the sea.

Anita remembers having a **(11)** .... as a pet.

Anita was inspired to become a conservationist by some

(12) .... she read.

Anita's first conservation job was in a **(13)** .... in Australia.

Anita's most memorable job in conservation involved working with

(14) .... , which are an endangered species in South Africa.

The aspect of her work that Anita finds most interesting is the

(15) .... of wild animals.

At the centre which Anita now runs, **(16)** ....

is the activity most popular amongst young people.

Teaching children how to recognise **(17)** ....

is something Anita thinks will be hard but enjoyable.

Anita says that going on **(18)** ....

is a good way for a young person to learn about a career as a conservationist.

Part 3

You will hear five short extracts in which teenagers are talking about taking photos on their phones. For questions **19–23**, choose from the list (**A–H**) the advice which each speaker gives. Use the letters only once. There are three extra letters which you do not need to use.

Listening test audio

A   Experiment with different subjects.

B   Take a large quantity of photos.

Speaker 1 [ ] **19**

C   Look closely at what's in the background.

Speaker 2 [ ] **20**

D   Consider how your photos will turn out.

Speaker 3 [ ] **21**

E   Use other people's work for inspiration.

Speaker 4 [ ] **22**

F   Consider different colour choices.

Speaker 5 [ ] **23**

G   Find out what the camera is capable of.

H   Use artificial lighting carefully.

Part 4

You will hear an interview with a man called Joe Newton, who dives off high places in a competitive sport known as cliff diving. For questions **24–30**, choose the best answer (**A**, **B** or **C**).

Listening test audio

24   What first attracted Joe to diving in a swimming pool?

    A   the opportunity it gave him to impress people

    B   the friendly attitude of some divers that he met

    C   the idea of doing something physically challenging

25   Why did Joe switch from pool diving to cliff diving?

    A   He thought he'd be more successful in competitions.

    B   He wanted to be able to dive in different places.

    C   He saw it as a way of making good money.

26   Joe says that the biggest difficulty when changing from pool diving to cliff diving is

    A   the way divers enter the water.

    B   the speed at which divers fall.

    C   the risks divers have to take.

27   When training, Joe wishes he could have

    A   more time to develop new types of dives.

    B   better access to practice facilities.

    C   more support from specialist coaches.

28   How did Joe feel about the last diving competition he took part in?

    A   annoyed about being interviewed straight after it

    B   disappointed with his performance in it

    C   concerned about the conditions in which it took place

29 Joe says that as he's diving down towards the water

    A he is unaware of his surroundings.

    B he feels a combination of fear and excitement.

    C he concentrates on getting the position of his body right.

30 What view does Joe express about the future of cliff diving?

    A Higher dives will be increasingly common.

    B More people will be encouraged to take up the sport.

    C Divers may be unable to meet fans' expectations.

Test 2

READING AND USE OF ENGLISH (1 hour 15 minutes)

Part 1

For questions **1–8**, read the text below and decide which answer (**A**, **B**, **C** or **D**) best fits each gap. There is an example at the beginning **(0)**.

Mark your answers on the separate answer sheet.

Example:

0 A resist   **B** fight   **C** endure   **D** oppose

0	A	B	C	D
	●	o	o	o

Why humans cannot help playing with their phones

Do you find it hard to **(0)** .... playing with your phone when chatting with friends? It is considered by some to be **(1)** .... manners, but a Cambridge psychoanalyst, Darian Leader, claims that holding and playing with objects is **(2)** .... new and humans actually do this so that they feel **(3)** .... during social interactions.

According to Leader, objects have always been used to **(4)** .... people's hands busy. In the 16th century, for example, people in Britain were criticised for their **(5)** .... to play with gloves and fans, or small boxes of tobacco, rather than talking to the person they were with.

Leader suggests that we should regard these objects as things which make human interactions possible. The objects **(6)** .... as a barrier and make it possible for us to **(7)** .... ourselves from the people around us. So our technology is a way of being with someone **(8)** .... at the same time, being somewhere else.

1   **A** low   **B** bad   **C** wrong   **D** rude

2   **A** little   **B** least   **C** nothing   **D** neither

3   **A** in comfort   **B** at ease   **C** with relief   **D** on top

4   **A** make   **B** hold   **C** leave   **D** keep

5   **A** tendency   **B** custom   **C** preference   **D** habit

6   **A** set   **B** form   **C** act   **D** constitute

7   **A** divide   **B** exclude   **C** split   **D** separate

8   **A** whether   **B** while   **C** unless   **D** except

Part 2

For questions **9–16**, read the text below and think of the word which best fits each gap. Use only **one** word in each gap. There is an example at the beginning **(0)**.

Write your answers **IN CAPITAL LETTERS on the separate answer sheet**.

Example: | 0 | | O | F | | | | | | | | | | | | | | |

Sweden's ice hotels

Sweden's *Icehotel* was built in 1989, 200 km north **(0)** .... the Arctic Circle. It is made entirely from blocks of something called 'snice', a mixture of ice and snow. **(9)** .... the fact that guests have to put **(10)** .... with the hotel's freezing -5°C temperature, *Icehotel* is extremely popular. Unfortunately, **(11)** .... is one problem: the blocks melt **(12)** .... year during the summer, and the hotel **(13)** .... to be completely rebuilt every winter.

Another hotel, called *Icehotel 365*, was built next to the original one in 2016. Although this hotel is also built entirely from ice, **(14)** .... is designed to remain open all year round. Thanks to solar panels fitted on the hotel's exterior, which prevent the sun's rays from reaching the icy structure, *Icehotel 365* remains frozen even during the summer months. Hans Eek, an architect **(15)** .... is an expert in sustainable building and was involved **(16)** .... the creation of this unique structure, says, 'Normally you build to keep the heat in, but we're building to keep the heat out.'

Part 3

For questions **17–24**, read the text below. Use the word given in capitals at the end of some of the lines to form a word that fits in the gap **in the same line**. There is an example at the beginning **(0)**.

Write your answers **IN CAPITAL LETTERS on the separate answer sheet**.

Example: **0** | C | O | N | C | L | U | S | I | O | N | | | | | | |

Can pet fish recognise their owners?

After studying a fish called the archerfish, scientists have reached
the **(0)** .... that fish may be able to distinguish between   **CONCLUDE**
people. This means that your pet fish could have many hidden
(17) .... and may even be able to recognise you in a crowd!   **ABLE**

Researchers   conducted   experiments   in   which,   to   their
(18) ...., archerfish were able to recall images of   **ASTONISH**
faces almost 81% of the time. And the **(19)** ....   **ACCURATE**
improved to 86% when the researchers thought they'd made the
(20) .... even harder, by replacing colour photos with   **IDENTIFY**
black and white images.

The discovery was so **(21)** .... because being able to   **EXPECT**
recognise human faces is a complex task, requiring a combination
of vision and memory. That's because we all have the same
(22) .... features and it is only small   **BASE**
(23) .... that distinguish humans from one another.   **DIFFERENT**
Scientists had always assumed that it was a skill possessed only by
those with **(24)** .... developed brains: humans and a few   **HIGH**
other animals, including horses, dogs, primates and some birds.

Part 4

For questions **25–30**, complete the second sentence so that it has a similar meaning to the first sentence, using the word given. **Do not change the word given.** You must use between **two** and **five** words, including the word given. Here is an example **(0)**.

Example:

0   Prizes are given out when the school year finishes.

   PLACE

   Prize-giving .... end of the school year.

The gap can be filled by the words 'takes place at the', so you write:

| **Example:** | **0** | *TAKES PLACE AT THE* |

Write **only** the missing words **IN CAPITAL LETTERS on the separate answer sheet**.

---

25   Your phone isn't here so I'm sure you left it at your grandmother's.

   MUST

   Your phone isn't here so .... it at your grandmother's.

26   Only use this door in an emergency.

   NOT

   This door is .... except in an emergency.

27   We didn't see that film because of the bad reviews.

   PUT

   The bad reviews .... that film.

28 I support the idea to ban cars from the city centre to reduce pollution.

FAVOUR

I am .... cars from the city centre to reduce pollution.

29 Don't lose this ticket as you must show it to staff at the museum.

ASKED

You'll .... your ticket to staff at the museum, so don't lose it.

30 Anna wouldn't share her sweets with her big brother.

PREPARED

Anna .... her sweets with her big brother.

Part 5

You are going to read an extract from a novel about a man called Alex, who with three other snowboarders, Dave, Hope and Bryce, is being trained to rescue people in the mountains. For questions **31–36**, choose the answer (**A**, **B**, **C** or **D**) which you think fits best according to the text.

Mark your answers on the separate answer sheet.

Snowboarders

The helicopter pitched forward, almost tossing me out of the open door. I grabbed the safety handle and pushed my goggles down over my eyes. There was a tap on my back. I turned around to see Dave waving at me to get out. In the front of the chopper, the copilot was making little circular motions with his hand. I knew what that meant: jump. The wind tossed the helicopter around and threw pellets of snow that felt like gravel on my face. I shifted my snowboard away from where I had it wedged against the door. The helicopter jerked backward again, and I held on to the safety handle with all my strength.

'Take a deep breath, Alex,' our instructor, Sam, said into my ear. I turned to look at him, and he smiled his big white smile. 'Now exhale.' I nodded. 'And then you just float out.' His hand drifted before him like a feather falling to earth. I nodded again, more confidently this time. Inhaled, like he had told me. Exhaled. 'Go, Alex,' Dave shouted. Dave had been heli-boarding half a dozen times. This was the first time I had ever even been in
line 25 a helicopter. Never mind jumping out of one.

I inched my board forward and let it dangle over the edge. The ground was thick and white, like a giant duvet. The rotor blades of the helicopter forced the snow up and out. It seemed like I was about to fall into a cloud. I wanted to jump, but you know what they say – the first step is the hardest. I inhaled again. Exhaled. Then I jumped. It felt like I was falling forever. When my board finally touched down, I bent my knees to soften the impact. It still made my spine shake and sent a shiver through my entire body. But at least I was on the ground. I hopped a couple of times to get going. Then I leaned into the downhill and pushed hard. I had never been up this high on

a mountain before. I did two quick turns, dug in hard on my toe edge and settled in beside Bryce and Hope.

'What took you so long?' Hope asked. 'My board got caught on the door.' The little bit of Hope's face that wasn't covered by pink tuque, goggles or neck warmer screwed up in a familiar way. 'You mean you got scared.' I pointed at the front of my board. 'It got stuck on the doorframe. I had to get it out. I didn't want to scrape up the bottom.' 'Seriously, Alex, how many rails did you do yesterday?' she said. 'And now you want me to believe you're suddenly all concerned about the bottom of your board?' 'Believe whatever you want, Hope.'

Bryce was the best non-professional snowboarder I had ever seen. When the rest of us were making big, jumpy turns down the hill, Bryce was cutting smooth lines. He was good – great even. But it was nothing to him. Just something he could do. I had spent the last two weeks training with Dave, Hope and Bryce. Dave was arrogant, but he didn't have the skills to back up his talk. I knelt down on the ground, my board out behind me, and let the cool breeze rush across my face. The helicopter was pitching in the wind. It went forward, then back, then a little higher, then down so low that it almost touched the ground. Suddenly Dave dropped out of the side. A moment later he was beside us, wiping snow from his goggles. 'Nice one,' Bryce said. Dave nodded as though he already knew it had been a nice jump. The helicopter pitched back again, then lifted up another twenty feet off the ground. 'What's happening?' I asked. Sam, our instructor and only connection to the rest of the world, was still on board.

31 Before he jumped out of the helicopter, Alex felt

   A concerned about the worsening weather.
   B grateful for his instructor's encouragement.
   C pleased he understood the copilot's instructions.
   D worried that there might be a problem with the helicopter.

32 Why does Alex use the words 'Never mind jumping out of one' in line 25?

   A to justify Dave's lack of patience with him
   B to explain why he was in the helicopter with Dave
   C to emphasise how unusual the situation was for him
   D to show he preferred to jump rather than stay in the helicopter

33 What does Alex suggest about his landing in the snow?

   A It was a relief despite being unpleasant.
   B It took him a while to recover from it.
   C He had forgotten the correct technique to use.
   D He was disappointed not to have done it better.

34 What does the conversation between Alex and Hope imply?

   A Hope never took any notice of what Alex said.
   B Hope was concerned for Alex's welfare.
   C Alex took pleasure in teasing Hope.
   D Alex did not get on well with Hope.

35 What do we learn about Dave in the final paragraph?

   A He recognised the need to improve his snowboarding skills.
   B He was more willing to take risks than the rest of the group.
   C He wasn't as good a snowboarder as he claimed to be.
   D He valued the compliments he received from Bryce.

36 How did Alex feel at the end of the extract?

   A disappointed at the group's change of plan
   B angry with Sam for not joining them
   C impatient to get moving again
   D anxious that they had been cut off

Part 6

You are going to read a magazine article about someone who goes on a trip to explore the bottom of the sea. Six sentences have been removed from the article. Choose from the sentences **A–G** the one which fits each gap (**37–42**). There is one extra sentence which you do not need to use.

Mark your answers on the separate answer sheet.

Ocean explorer

I'm on a speedboat with some research scientists off the southern coast of Bermuda in the North Atlantic Ocean. A crew member points to a spot on our speedboat's GPS screen. The location is surrounded by red flags and carries a warning in bold text: 'This area is to be avoided'. 'And that's exactly where we're heading,' he announces cheerfully. We're going there to meet the Baseline Explorer research ship. For the last month, it has circled Bermuda, sending people down in small underwater craft called 'submersibles', to depths of up to 200 metres.

Today, I'm going down in one of these submersibles to investigate an area that, like 95% of the seabed, is totally unexplored. The research is part of an ongoing global campaign to examine what life is like in the ocean's depths. **37** The survey techniques used in the study can be shared with researchers making their own measurements. This is part of the development of a standard method that any oceanographer and marine biologist can apply.

After a quick safety briefing, I take off my shoes and slide into the submersible to sit beside the pilot. We are going to explore a particular area of the seabed in detail. **38** It is uncomfortably hot. I can see in all directions through the transparent sides and floor.

A crane lifts our submersible into the air and deposits us in the sea. The pilot runs through a series of checks over the radio: the batteries aren't leaking, the engines are working, and the life systems are good. I give the 'OK' sign to a man on the deck of the ship, confirming that I don't mind spending time in this tiny space. **39**

Our vessel slips under the surface, tipping forward and then becoming upright again. For the next half hour, we drift downward. **40** What I'm even less prepared for is the sheer vastness of the ocean and I'm excited at the thought of how mysterious it still is.

At 200 metres deep, the pilot suddenly points. **41** As we move along at a leisurely one metre per second towards it, we spot a variety of colourful fish all around us, including some butterfly fish darting between the rocks. A pair of lionfish also pop up, then disappear into the darkness.

Ahead of us, another craft is filming part of the ocean floor. A team of scientists will examine the videos, counting the different species they see. **42** Other submersibles return with actual samples of the local wildlife: sea stars, crabs, urchins and coral. After a couple of hours, we finally hit the surface again, a little bit wiser about the alien world below.

A	Once that reassurance is communicated, we are given official permission to begin our dive.	**E**	So far, five or six new ones have been discovered, as well as a handful of fish that couldn't immediately be identified.
B	To my surprise, the water fades rapidly from clear green to a rather murky blue-black, reducing the visibility considerably.	**F**	The goal is to carry out an 'ocean health check', helping us to understand not only what this ecosystem looks like now, but how it is changing over time.
C	At the centre of the gleaming yellow craft is a glass dome, just big enough for two passengers to squeeze into.	**G**	At first I'm not sure why but then, just ahead of us, an enormous submerged mountain gradually appears.
D	Such a breakthrough would clearly depend on similar technological advances.		

Part 7

You are going to read magazine article about young people learning to play the cello. For questions **43–52**, choose from the people (**A–D**). The people may be chosen more than once.

Mark your answers on the separate answer sheet.

Which person

says that a key requirement for playing is difficult under certain conditions?   **43** [ ]

admits the difficulties of playing can negatively affect how they feel about the cello?   **44** [ ]

took considerable time to realise how they truly felt about the instrument?   **45** [ ]

attempted to overcome what they felt was a lack of talent by trying hard?   **46** [ ]

mentions their impatience to make progress?   **47** [ ]

says a cello can reveal a great deal about the person playing it?   **48** [ ]

took up the cello as the result of the limited options available?   **49** [ ]

was disappointed by the inability of skilled cellists to explain their technique?   **50** [ ]

mentions the gap between what players can do, and what they often aspire to?   **51** [ ]

believes that too few people appreciate how good the cello can sound?   **52** [ ]

Learning to play the cello

A Sophie

I love playing the cello. It's such a large instrument, it forces you to embrace it as you play. And because it vibrates, it almost feels as if it's alive and breathing; to me, the sound is often close to that of someone singing. It really allows the player to express their personality, too. It's almost as though the listeners can hear the musician's soul. Having said all that, there are times when I find it an intensely annoying and frustrating instrument – when I haven't played for a while and I start practising again, and just can't get my fingers into exactly the right position, the resulting sounds can be really screechy and awful. But I love its diversity, and I wish it was more widely heard. Although it's sometimes used in TV ads, that's not enough for the general public to realise what wonderful music the cello can make.

B Josh

I could already play the guitar by the time I started the cello, and I chose it because I thought that restricting myself to string instruments would make things easy for me. In fact there were endless frustrations initially, as it seemed I'd become a lot worse as a musician. I knew what great music should sound like, and the noises I was producing weren't even close. As a result, I began practising obsessively in any moment I had. I loved the instrument, but I realised I wasn't a natural cellist. I was determined not to let that stand in my way, though. Another frustration was that if I asked any professional cellist exactly how they played, they were unable to describe what was physically needed to achieve the beautiful tone I was looking for. So for me, it seemed to be down to trial and error – and I was desperate to improve quickly!

C Liam

I love the cello, and after loads of lessons, I've come to terms with the fact that although it's dead easy for teachers who've been playing for years to draw the bow smoothly across the strings of the instrument and make a beautiful sound, they forget that for beginners to achieve that requires a level of control that's usually beyond them. Doing it wrong produces a scratchy note that'll make your audience screw up their faces in pain. Until you can do it properly, your playing will always sound poor, and you'll be light years from playing the sort of music that probably attracted you to the instrument in the first place. And teachers always stress how important it is to relax your arms and upper body – but how on earth can you, when you're approaching a piece of music you have zero chance of getting through without a mistake? But I'm hoping that'll come with increased competence!

D Karen

I wish I could say I'd wanted to play the cello ever since I heard it on TV or something. The truth is, I began for one reason only: the choice was between the violin and cello, as these were the only instruments we had at home, and my mother decided I looked ridiculous holding the violin – although how I could have looked less strange playing an instrument twice my size, I'll never know. It wasn't until after tons of lessons and countless nerve-racking concert appearances with my school orchestra that it struck me I'd actually fallen in love with the instrument; it had just taken me until then to see it. The cello can produce the richest and warmest tones in music. And for me, it's also one of the most versatile of the string instruments, able to produce notes that are unbelievably high, and yet just a moment later, sink down into the depths and cause the room to vibrate with its lowest notes. Fabulous!

WRITING (1 hour 20 minutes)

Part 1

You **must** answer this question. Write your answer in **140–190** words in an appropriate style on the separate answer sheet.

---

1   In your English class you have been talking about school trips. Now your English teacher has asked you to write an essay for homework.

Write your essay using **all** the notes and giving reasons for your point of view.

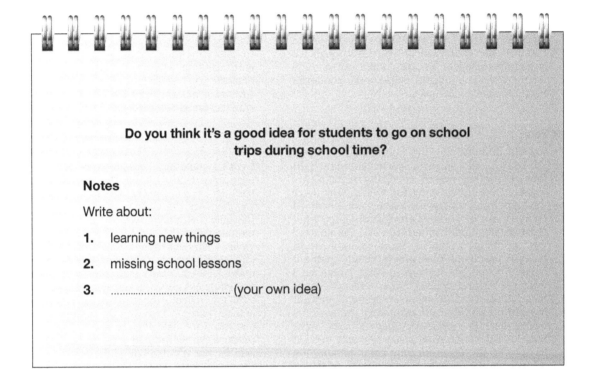

Do you think it's a good idea for students to go on school trips during school time?

Notes

Write about:

1.   learning new things

2.   missing school lessons

3.   .... (your own idea)

Part 2

Write an answer to **one** of the questions **2–4** in this part. Write your answer in **140–190** words in an appropriate style on the separate answer sheet. Put the question number in the box at the top of the answer sheet.

---

2   You recently saw this notice on a sports website.

> *Reviews wanted*
>
> **A good place to do sports**
>
> Do you know a really good place in your area where teenagers can do sports? It could be a sports centre, a gym, a club, or your local park.
>
> Tell us about the place, explain what's good and bad about it and say whether you'd recommend it to other teenagers.
>
> The best reviews will be published next month.

Write your **review**.

3   You receive this email from your English friend, Eliza.

> Hi!
>
> Next year I have to decide whether to study history or geography at school. Actually I enjoy both subjects, but I can only do one on my timetable. I don't know which subject to choose. I'd really like some advice.
>
> Many thanks
>
> Eliza

Write your **email**.

4   You see this advert in an English language magazine for teenagers.

> *Articles wanted*
>
> **It was OK in the end!**
>
> Have you ever done anything that was difficult, but which ended well? Tell us about it and explain how you felt afterwards.
>
> The best article will be published in the magazine.

Write your **article**.

LISTENING (approximately 40 minutes)

Part 1

You will hear people talking in eight different situations.
For questions **1–8**, choose the best answer (**A**, **B** or **C**).

Listening test audio

1   You hear a young man talking about a trip to a historic site.

     What aspect of the trip disappointed him?

     A the quality of the guided tour

     B the condition of the old buildings

     C the unexpectedly poor weather

2   You hear a teenage girl telling a friend about a book she has read.

     Why is she unsure whether to recommend it to him?

     A The element of fantasy might not appeal to him.

     B He might find the main character irritating.

     C There might not be enough action in it for him.

3   You hear part of a programme about amber, a natural material used in some jewellery.

     What is the speaker's purpose?

     A to describe why amber is so popular in jewellery

     B to inform people about where amber can be found

     C to explain why one piece of amber was special

4   You hear a boy telling his friend about his brother's job.

     What is the boy doing?

     A describing the benefits of the job

     B giving advice on how to get the job

     C explaining why his brother gets discouraged by the job

5   You hear two students talking about a history lecture they've been to.

What do they both think about it?

   A   The delivery was less interesting than they'd hoped.

   B   Their preparation turned out to be essential.

   C   It was impossible for them to understand.

6   You hear a boy telling his friend about his volleyball final next weekend.

How does he feel about the match?

   A   confident that his team has a good chance of winning

   B   concerned about how well their opponents will play

   C   surprised at how much interest there is in it

7   You hear a girl telling a friend about a pencil museum she visited.

What surprised her about the museum?

   A   how interesting she found it

   B   how attractive the displays were

   C   how popular it was with visitors

8   You hear a teacher telling her class about a science competition their school took part in.

What is she doing?

   A   giving students advice for future science experiments

   B   congratulating the winning team on their unusual choice of topic

   C   encouraging students to take more interest in science experiments

Part 2

You will hear a boy called Mark giving a class presentation about a mountain biking trip he went on. For questions **9–18**, complete the sentences with a word or short phrase.

Listening test audio

Mountain biking in Scotland

Mark and his father met their mountain biking group outside a **(9)** .... near a town called Fort William.

Mark hadn't realised how **(10)** .... a mountain bike could be.

Mark found the **(11)** .... on the bike hard to get used to at first.

Mark fell off his bike in the forest, when he ran into a large **(12)** ....

Mark was surprised to hear that **(13)** .... had once lived in the forest.

At the hostel where his group spent the night, a story about a **(14)** .... made a big impression on Mark.

On the second morning, **(15)** .... on the track meant Mark had to get off the bike and walk.

Mark describes seeing a large bird in the sky as a good **(16)** .... during one tough part of the ride.

Apart from some **(17)** ...., the weather was fine during the ride.

The final part of the ride was along a path running next to a **(18)** ....

Part 3

You will hear five short extracts in which teenagers are talking about a free time activity they have given up. For questions **19–23**, choose from the list (**A–H**) why each speaker gave up the activity. Use the letters only once. There are three extra letters which you do not need to use.

Listening test audio

A   I wanted to try a related activity.

B   I believed I was too old for it.

| Speaker 1 | | 19 |

C   It became too expensive.

| Speaker 2 | | 20 |

D   It required too much commitment.

| Speaker 3 | | 21 |

E   I didn't have enough time to do it.

| Speaker 4 | | 22 |

F   I became bored with it.

| Speaker 5 | | 23 |

G   I stopped making progress.

H   I felt isolated from people I knew.

Part 4

You will hear an interview with a student called Daniella Masters, talking about a day she spent with a professional wildlife photographer called John Baker. For questions **24–30**, choose the best answer (**A**, **B** or **C**).

Listening test audio

---

24   According to John Baker, most people don't manage to take great wildlife photos because

   A   they're too easily satisfied with poor-quality shots.

   B   they don't bother to prepare their equipment.

   C   they have too little experience of being outdoors.

25   How did Daniella feel after trying to photograph an otter?

   A   pleased about the photo she took instead

   B   disappointed that she'd missed a rare opportunity

   C   concerned for the creature's welfare

26   Daniella learnt that to film some waterbirds, she'd have to

   A   prepare for a long wait in a shelter to spot them.

   B   be ready to get some fast shots of them.

   C   encourage them to come close enough.

27   When talking about her camera, Daniella admits that

   A   she'd assumed she needed better accessories for it.

   B   she'd been unaware of some of the functions it had.

   C   she'd never experimented with the settings on it.

28   What does Daniella say about her photos of a swan?

   A   She could see major improvements after guidance from John.

   B   She was proud of them in spite of John's comments.

   C   She realised she kept making the same basic mistakes.

29 At the coast, Daniella and John managed to

    A obtain some very natural pictures of seals.

    B approach some seals without frightening them.

    C locate more seals than they had expected.

30 At the end of her day with John, Daniella was

    A doubtful whether she could ever achieve John's level of skill.

    B aware she needed to observe wildlife more carefully.

    C struggling to remember everything she'd been taught.

Test 3

READING AND USE OF ENGLISH (1 hour 15 minutes)

Part 1

For questions **1–8**, read the text below and decide which answer (**A**, **B**, **C** or **D**) best fits each gap. There is an example at the beginning **(0)**.

Mark your answers on the separate answer sheet.

Example:

0 A located   **B** positioned   **C** placed   **D** set

0	A	B	C	D
	●	o	o	o

Space research on Devon Island

Devon Island, **(0)** .... in Canada's Northern Arctic region, is the largest uninhabited island in the world. However, that is not the only reason why it is famous – it is also known for the research **(1)** .... out there by the US space agency NASA, **(2)** .... others. Devon Island is isolated, the environment is harsh, and the area is poorly mapped, which makes it the perfect place to get a **(3)** .... of what it might be like to live and work on Mars.

Researchers **(4)** .... in particular on a geological feature called the Haughton Crater. This area, 23 km in diameter, has almost no vegetation and the temperature **(5)** .... well below zero for most of the year. **(6)** .... , very little erosion has occurred here, and the surface of the land **(7)** .... resembles that seen on Mars. Researchers have used the area to test robots, spacesuits, drills and other tools that would **(8)** .... future Mars explorers. They have also taken the opportunity to assess the skills of potential Mars colonists.

1	**A**	worked	**B**	turned	**C**	taken	**D**	carried
2	**A**	besides	**B**	among	**C**	between	**D**	above
3	**A**	sample	**B**	taste	**C**	bite	**D**	trial
4	**A**	focus	**B**	search	**C**	aim	**D**	examine
5	**A**	lasts	**B**	remains	**C**	continues	**D**	stands
6	**A**	Literally	**B**	Similarly	**C**	Alternatively	**D**	Consequently
7	**A**	closely	**B**	directly	**C**	strictly	**D**	narrowly
8	**A**	advise	**B**	contribute	**C**	aid	**D**	promote

Part 2

For questions **9–16**, read the text below and think of the word which best fits each gap. Use only **one** word in each gap. There is an example at the beginning **(0)**.

Write your answers **IN CAPITAL LETTERS on the separate answer sheet**.

Example: | **0** | *T* | *O* | | | | | | | | | | | | | | | | |

Alcock and Brown

In 1919, two British men, John Alcock and Arthur Whitten Brown, were the first people **(0)** .... fly by plane across the Atlantic. They took **(9)** .... from Canada and crash-landed sixteen hours **(10)** .... in the west of Ireland.

They flew through cloud, fog, rain and snow. At **(11)** .... point an exhaust pipe broke and burst **(12)** .... flames. Then their air speed indicator stopped working. Often they flew dangerously **(13)** .... to the surface of the ocean in **(14)** .... to stop ice forming on the plane. Despite the danger, Brown even went out on the wings on six occasions to remove some ice.

Many wrongly believe Charles Lindberg's far more famous flight from New York to Paris in 1927 was the first transatlantic flight. But in fact his achievement was to do it solo. The distance flown by Alcock and Brown, 3,040 km, was barely half that flown by Lindberg. Nevertheless, their flight ought **(15)** .... go down in history because it was the first time that anyone **(16)** .... flown across the Atlantic.

Part 3

For questions **17–24**, read the text below. Use the word given in capitals at the end of some of the lines to form a word that fits in the gap **in the same line**. There is an example at the beginning **(0)**.

Write your answers **IN CAPITAL LETTERS on the separate answer sheet.**

Example: | 0 | P | I | A | N | I | S | T | | | | | | | | |

Franz Liszt (1811–1886)

Franz Liszt was a Hungarian **(0)** .... and composer. He was particularly well-known for his creativity. Taught by his father, he was giving public **(17)** .... in concert halls by the age of nine.   **PIANO**

   PERFORM

His most impressive talent was his ability to improvise an original **(18)** .... from a tune suggested by a member of his audience. Encouraged by his success, father and son travelled to Vienna. Many great composers lived in this Austrian city, making it the perfect place for an **(19)** .... young musician.   **COMPOSE**

   AMBITION

As an adult, Liszt toured throughout Europe. He pleased audiences with his likeable **(20)** .... and incredible technique. His travels provided him with inspiration for his music. However, many of the pieces he wrote are **(21)** .... difficult to play, and very few pianists can perform them properly. At the time, some people **(22)** .... of Liszt's approach to music, but this negative **(23)** .... did not affect his popularity. Many pupils asked for his **(24)** .... , and he trained some of the top musicians of his day.   **PERSON**

   EXTRAORDINARY

   APPROVE

   CRITIC

   GUIDE

Part 4

For questions **25–30**, complete the second sentence so that it has a similar meaning to the first sentence, using the word given. **Do not change the word given.** You must use between **two** and **five** words, including the word given. Here is an example **(0)**.

Example:

0   Prizes are given out when the school year finishes.

   PLACE

   Prize-giving ………………………………………………… end of the school year.

The gap can be filled by the words 'takes place at the', so you write:

Example:	0	*TAKES PLACE AT THE*

Write **only** the missing words **IN CAPITAL LETTERS on the separate answer sheet**.

---

25   I think it was silly of you not to ask Mary to help you with your homework.

   SHOULD

   I think …………………………………………… Mary to help you with your homework.

26   Even if I train very hard, I never seem to win any races.

   NO

   I never seem to win any races …………………………………………… hard I train.

27   'Where did you find such a great diagram?' the teacher asked me.

   HAD

   The teacher asked me …………………………………………… such a great diagram.

28 We need to talk to Kate about the party.

WORD

We need to .... Kate about the party.

29 We didn't visit the castle because we ran out of time.

MORE

If we'd .... definitely have visited the castle.

30 I was annoyed because Lucy didn't make the effort to tell me she was going to be late.

BOTHERED

It annoyed me that Lucy couldn't .... me know she was going to be late.

Part 5

You are going to read an article about board games. For questions **31–36**, choose the answer (**A**, **B**, **C** or **D**) which you think fits best according to the text.

Mark your answers on the separate answer sheet.

Board games

Dan Jolin reports on a type of board game called 'Eurogames'.

John and Zuzi Morgan have set up a café in Oxford, in the UK, where people can not only enjoy a cup of coffee and some cake but play a board game too. The owners' hope is that people enjoy the experience so much they want to repeat it. Zuzi explains why they decided to turn their love of tabletop games into a full-time business: 'There's so much technology. Everybody's busy and you want to bring people back together in a way that's not just staring at screens. It's a natural thing in people. We're supposed to be together and communicating with each other.' The games played in John and Zuzi's café are known as 'Eurogames' which have gentle themes, such as farming and landscape-building.

The first game of this type was *The Settlers of Catan* created by a German designer, Klaus Teuber. Players competitively establish settlements on an island and trade resources with the other players, keeping participants fully engaged and sustaining the drama of the narrative right to the conclusion, with none *line 23* of the players feeling left out. That crucial factor was refined in the 'co-operative' games that followed, in which every player wins or loses as a team member, provoking a lot more social interaction.

Pandemic, a Eurogame in which players must collaborate to solve global problems, was created by an American, Matt Leacock, one of tabletop gaming's most successful designers. Leacock's passion for board games goes back to his experience of frustration with them as a child. 'Games were my favourite birthday gift,' he says, 'but I'd get very excited, open up the box, then we'd play and there would just be crushing disappointment.' So, with the help of a game-enthusiast uncle, young Leacock would flip over the boards of the many games they played together and try to design something better using the same components.

Pandemic was a runaway success, and the follow-up version represented another leap forward in game design. 'It incorporates,' Leacock explains, 'a tremendous amount of storytelling. It's similar to an electronic game in that you develop your characters, you get new rules and the state of the world changes.' As he says, 'it is an unfolding story.' *line 49*

The growth of the video games industry has, perhaps contrary to expectations, been one of the biggest factors in the success of these modern board games – largely because the presence of games consoles under so many TVs and the rise of mobile gaming have normalised game-playing. 'Video games and board games have learned an awful lot from each other,' says Ben Hogg, who works for a leading games company. 'Everyone's a mobile gamer now. Speak to anyone who's got a smartphone, they've got at least one game they like to play on it'.

For a time, video-gaming offered a level of physical social interaction, at the arcade or through multi-player sofa games that people could play together in the same room. Then multi-player video games moved online, and fellow players became physically removed from one another, if not completely anonymous. So, some people who had previously enjoyed playing video games started looking for a way of playing games again with other people who were physically present. As is evident in John and Zuzi's busy and popular café, tabletop gaming has become more than entertainment. In our increasingly online society, games have become something to be shared, directly and physically, in the real world and this trend is set to continue.

31 What does Zuzi Morgan say about the board game café?

    A Once people have been there, they tend to return regularly.
    B Its appeal to customers lies in its originality.
    C Technology is sometimes a distraction there.
    D It satisfies a basic human need.

32 What does the phrase 'That crucial factor' refer to in lines 23–24?

    A all players being part of a team
    B the option of playing a series of games
    C every player being involved all the time
    D the excitement of meeting other players

33 What do we learn about Matt Leacock's childhood?

    A He hated losing when playing board games.
    B His uncle introduced him to a wide variety of games.
    C The games he was given failed to live up to his expectations.
    D The games he received as presents were rarely what he had asked for.

34 What is meant by 'unfolding' in line 49?

    A evolving
    B innovative
    C absorbing
    D predictable

35 What point is made in the fifth paragraph about new types of board game?

    A Those inspired by video games are becoming widespread.
    B Their popularity is partly due to people's familiarity with video games.
    C Players find them attractive because they enjoy a change from video games.
    D They often require players to use skills developed through playing video games.

36 In the final paragraph, the writer suggests that

    A board games make up for something that modern video games lack.
    B there may be a renewed interest in video games in the future.
    C many people would rather play board games in cafés than at home.
    D video games became less challenging when people started playing online.

Part 6

You are going to read an article about some ancient ships discovered in the Black Sea. Six sentences have been removed from the article. Choose from the sentences **A–G** the one which fits each gap (**37–42**). There is one extra sentence which you do not need to use.

Mark your answers on the separate answer sheet.

Ancient ships in the Black Sea

In 2016, an international team of researchers from the University of Southampton in the UK made an amazing discovery in the Black Sea – the sea between Eastern Europe and Western Asia. The goal of their expedition had been to map the sea floor and study the prehistoric landscapes, which were flooded during the last ice age. To their surprise, they came across perfectly preserved shipwrecks – ships that had sunk to the bottom of the sea a long time ago.

Many of the 41 wrecks they found were already known about from historical sources. **37 |_____|** They were dispersed across roughly 2,000 square kilometres and were discovered during a month-long survey conducted by the scientists aboard the research ship, Stril Explorer. The ships, which were lying between 150 and 2,200 metres beneath the surface of the water, were in such perfect condition that researchers could make out individual rope coils, rudders, pots and wooden decorative elements. Even marks made by tools on specific planks were visible.

The oldest ship found dates back to the late 800s when the region was part of the Byzantine Empire. There are also numerous Ottoman vessels from the 16th to the 18th centuries as well as a few from the 19th century. **38 |_____|** It turned out to be the remains of a 14th century medieval Italian vessel, dating from the days of Marco Polo, the famous explorer from Venice.

Images of the sunken ships were captured by high resolution 3D cameras. **39 |_____|** Information from the pictures taken gave them an idea of each ship's starting port and also where it was probably heading. Because the crafts were found quite far out to sea, experts believed they were merchant trading ships travelling over great distances.

Finding such well-preserved wrecks is a very rare occurrence, as wood and rope usually break down rapidly in saltwater. **40 |_____|** It was once a freshwater lake, although that changed about 12,000 years ago, at the end of the last ice age. As temperatures rose, they caused water levels in the nearby Mediterranean Sea to rise, and saltwater began entering the lake.

As a result, the Black Sea is now fed by saltwater, as well as freshwater from rivers. The two types of water have different amounts of salt in them, creating distinct regions of water. The upper layer, with less salt in it, contains oxygen, while the water that lies 150 metres below the surface contains none. Oxygen breaks down natural materials, so without it, things like ropes and wood disintegrate at a much slower rate. Also, the inhospitable environment means there are no tiny animals to feed on the materials. **41 |_____|**

Given that the Black Sea was the site of most of the ancient Greek, Roman and Byzantine Empire's colonial and commercial activities, marine archaeologists say the discovery provided interesting information about trading habits and community life during those times. **42 |_____|** In fact most ships were merchant transports carrying goods like grain, timber and other commodities.

A   However, that didn't happen in this case because the Black Sea is a little different from other seas.

B   Nevertheless, they were able to use the best technology available to find them.

C   While these ships were interesting, there was one from a different period which was particularly exciting.

D   Although learning more about such things makes the wrecks historically valuable, no-one ever expected to find any treasure.

E   However, none of them had ever been seen before.

F   These factors, taken together, explain why the ships had been so well preserved.

G   Marine archaeologists had fitted these onto remotely operated underwater vehicles.

Part 7

You are going to read an article in which four people talk about the sport they do. For questions **43–52**, choose from the people (**A–D**). The people may be chosen more than once.

Mark your answers on the separate answer sheet.

Which person

says how overcoming a fear has proved worthwhile?	43
says they constantly think ahead while doing their sport?	44
compares actually performing an action to practising for it?	45
mentions being unfamiliar with some aspects of their sport at first?	46
mentions the mental focus required to do their sport?	47
emphasises how much potential there is for problems to occur?	48
has ambitions to do their sport in a wide variety of locations?	49
enjoys someone's company while doing their sport?	50
says their sport is organised in a similar way to another sport?	51
emphasises the freedom they experience when doing their sport?	52

Four sportspeople

A Gary, surfer

Every wave is different, and there are waves out there, all over the world, that I intend to ride. To catch a wave, you have to position yourself behind the white water. You start paddling as a wave approaches and, just before it breaks, jump up to your feet. Getting from a paddling position, lying on your stomach, to standing on the board in one smooth motion takes a good degree of skill. But it's easier to do this in the sea than when you're a beginner training on dry land, as you can use the momentum of the water to your advantage. The feeling when you step off the land into the sea, into an untamed and wild environment, is amazing. The speed, the power and the G-force as you do huge sweeping and swooping turns off the top of the wave is about as close as you can get to flying. It's addictive.

B Stephanie, flat-water kayaker

One day, some talent spotters came to my school and tested the sporty people in my year. My friend and I both got a letter saying we'd been selected for flat-water kayaking. I'd done a bit of kayaking on holiday, but I never knew it was a competitive sport nor how physically demanding it could be. Flat-water kayaking takes place anywhere with a long stretch of water, much like the Olympic rowing events. In a sprint, you line up in one of nine lanes, then go as fast as you can in a straight line for either 200, 500 or 1,000 metres. The racing kayaks are long, sleek and about the width of your hips. They're also rather unstable, so there is, of course, the possibility of capsizing. Apart from wanting to win, the main draw is the social side. You see the same faces at competitions, and I've made friends with people from all over the country.

C Amy, rock climber

Generally speaking, there are two types of outdoor climbing: sport climbing, where there are metal bolts in the rock that you clip into as you go up to keep safe, and traditional climbing. The latter is where you place your own bits of equipment in the rock as you climb, to catch you if you fall. My cousin introduced me to the sport and I really took to it. The adrenaline rush is part of the appeal. Climbing is the ultimate full-body workout, and there's nothing like it for living in the moment. You're out on this cliff, exposed to the wind and freezing weather: you can't afford to worry about other things in your life because you really have to concentrate on keeping yourself safe. When I started, I didn't like to look down, but over time and with some effort, I've become less anxious so now I've really started to appreciate my surroundings. I've seen some places that other people don't often get to see, and from a totally unique perspective.

D Jim, track cyclist

My dad's a keen track cyclist too and we race against each other. We compete in the same league every Friday. I usually do better than him but sometimes he'll beat me. It's just nice to be able to race alongside him. Riding inside a velodrome is very different from cycling on the road. The tracks have incredibly steep sides, known as the banking. When you're at the top, you're almost horizontal – I found it a bit scary at first. You're always at the limit of how hard you can go, always planning your next move. And there are any number of mishaps that can happen, especially as the bikes don't have brakes – you can only slow down by pushing back against the pedals or going up the banking. Towards the end of a race, your legs feel as if they're on fire.

WRITING (1 hour 20 minutes)

Part 1

You **must** answer this question. Write your answer in **140–190** words in an appropriate style on the separate answer sheet.

1   In your English class you have been talking about wasting things. Now your English teacher has asked you to write an essay.

Write your essay using **all** the notes and giving reasons for your point of view.

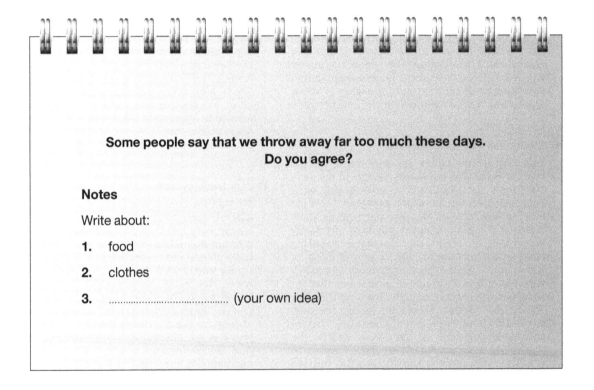

**Some people say that we throw away far too much these days.
Do you agree?**

Notes

Write about:

1.   food

2.   clothes

3.   .... (your own idea)

Part 2

Write an answer to **one** of the questions **2–4** in this part. Write your answer in **140–190** words in an appropriate style on the separate answer sheet. Put the question number in the box at the top of the answer sheet.

---

2   You see this advert in an international magazine for teenagers.

> *Articles wanted*
>
> ## School life
>
> What things make school life interesting and what can make it boring? How could school life be improved in your opinion?
>
> The best articles will be published in the magazine.

Write your **article**.

3   You recently saw this notice in an English magazine.

> *Reviews wanted*
>
> ## Swimming pools
>
> Is there a swimming pool which you particularly like? If so, write a review describing the pool, its facilities, and the staff who work there. Explain why you would recommend the pool to other people.
>
> We will post the best reviews.

Write your **review**.

4   Your teacher has asked you to write a story for the school English magazine.

> ## Stories wanted
>
> Your story must begin with this sentence:
>
> *Jack and Pedro were trekking through the mountains on the first day of their holidays.*
>
> Your story must include:
>
> * black clouds
> * a cave

Write your **story**.

LISTENING (approximately 40 minutes)

Part 1

You will hear people talking in eight different situations.
For questions **1–8**, choose the best answer (**A**, **B** or **C**).

Listening test audio

1 You hear a young photographer who has just taken part in an international photography competition.

How does she feel about the photographs she entered for the competition?

A proud that they were so unusual

B pleased that her parents approved of them

C hopeful that they will have an impact

2 You hear a science teacher talking to his students about research into an ancient volcanic eruption.

What is he trying to do?

A explain to them the possible problems of the methods used

B show them how much evidence is needed to establish a fact

C tell them how to check the results of their experiments

3 You hear two friends talking about football.

How does the girl feel about what the boy says?

A unsure about whether to believe him

B surprised by his knowledge of the subject

C confused by some of the details he mentions

4 You hear a boy telling a friend about an ice festival he went to.

What did he enjoy most about it?

A having the opportunity to do some activities on ice

B learning how to make things out of ice

C listening to a concert in an ice castle

5 You hear a girl talking about playing tennis in international competitions.

What does she say about the other players?

A She tries to get on well with them because she has no choice.

B Her relationships with them improve when she is playing well.

C They make friendships based on understanding each other's problems.

6 You hear part of an interview with a girl who took part in an extreme marathon.

What is she doing?

A expressing gratitude for the support she received

B justifying her decision to take part in the race

C describing her relief that nothing went wrong

7 You hear two friends discussing a news story about a wild animal.

How does the girl feel about the story?

A concerned about what it might mean for the animal

B surprised at the interest it has attracted

C uncertain about how true it is

8 You hear a teacher giving feedback to his students about their written homework.

How does he feel about the students' work?

A annoyed that it was left incomplete

B disappointed with their attitude towards it

C dissatisfied with the standard of presentation

Part 2

You will hear a man called Alan James talking about his work as a stuntman, performing the extreme action scenes in films, in place of the main actor. For questions **9–18**, complete the sentences with a word or short phrase.

Listening test audio

Alan James, action scene specialist

Alan suggests that action scenes taking place on **(9)** .... have become his speciality.

Alan says that thanks to the approach known as **(10)** .... , action scenes are as safe as they can be.

Alan says the feelings he has before an action scene are due to

(11) ....

Alan believes his choice of career was decided when he started riding a

(12) ....

Alan says the lack of **(13)** .... is a problem for people wishing to work in the industry.

Alan gives the example of **(14)** .... as a skill he's reached the top level in.

Alan says the majority of people like him work as **(15)** .... to build up enough screen experience for the job.

Alan thinks his most thrilling action scene was flying a **(16)** .... in poor weather conditions.

One scene that Alan wasn't keen on involved having a **(17)** .... with an actor.

In Alan's opinion, the film called **(18)** .... best shows his work.

Part 3

You will hear five short extracts in which teenagers are talking about weekend courses they have been doing. For questions **19–23**, choose from the list (**A–H**) what each speaker appreciates most about the course. Use the letters only once. There are three extra letters which you do not need to use.

Listening test audio

A   the opportunity to be creative

B   the patience of the instructor

Speaker 1 [ ] 19

C   the clear objectives that were set

Speaker 2 [ ] 20

D   the emphasis on practical activities

Speaker 3 [ ] 21

E   the respect gained by learning a particular skill

Speaker 4 [ ] 22

F   the difference from usual school work

Speaker 5 [ ] 23

G   the enthusiasm of fellow learners

H   the flexibility of the timetable

Part 4

You will hear an interview with a young woman called Laura Wilson, a dancer who gave up dancing and decided to write a book. For questions **24–30**, choose the best answer (**A**, **B** or **C**).

Listening test audio

24 Laura says that when she was studying at dance school she

    A found it difficult to adjust to the strict routine at first.

    B was concerned that she hadn't established her career.

    C came to regard the discipline as a natural way of life.

25 How did Laura feel about giving up dancing?

    A She regretted not having opportunities to perform.

    B She was relieved that she'd have no further physical problems.

    C She accepted the fact that she was not good enough.

26 According to Laura, she chose to write a book because she

    A hoped to provide practical help to young dancers.

    B felt she could write well for children.

    C understood that it was the best option for her own skills.

27 Why did Laura include the dancer called Karen Jonson in her book?

    A to illustrate what it's like to be part of a dance company

    B to clarify the difficulties some dancers face early in their careers

    C to highlight the importance of a balanced attitude towards dance

28 How does Laura feel about the qualities professional dancers display?

    A She envies their determination.

    B She dislikes their attitude towards criticism.

    C She admires their ability to stay motivated at all times.

29 Laura made up her mind to write about the possibility of failure in her book

    A to demonstrate the most common reasons for it.

    B to show how people can use it positively.

    C to explain how it causes some dancers to give up before they should.

30 What does Laura want the main message of her book to be?

    A Dancers should try to get the parts that suit them.

    B Dancers need to be lucky in order to achieve success.

    C Dancers have to use social media in order to get noticed.

Test 4

READING AND USE OF ENGLISH (1 hour 15 minutes)

Part 1

For questions **1–8**, read the text below and decide which answer (**A**, **B**, **C** or **D**) best fits each gap. There is an example at the beginning **(0)**.

Mark your answers on the separate answer sheet.

Example:

0   **A** barely   **B** only   **C** nearly   **D** simply

0	A	B	C	D
	●	o	o	o

What do birds 'say' to each other?

You're undoubtedly so used to hearing birds singing and calling out to each other that you **(0)** .... pause to think about what the sounds they're making really mean. You may be **(1)** .... that calls are used for different purposes, perhaps to signal a predator is close by, provide information to other birds about the location of a food **(2)** .... or to defend territory. But how can you **(3)** .... what message is being conveyed?

Birds don't use words in the way humans do, but like us, they **(4)** .... emotionally to different situations by using these different calls to communicate with each other. **(5)** .... you're in a place where you don't speak the local language and someone screams or shouts out. You would understand whether that person was scared or excited simply from the tone of their voice.

Bird calls seem to function in a very similar **(6)** .... For example, bird calls are soft when birds are calm or feeding, and loud and aggressive when they're under **(7)** .... Listen carefully, and these differences will help you **(8)** .... out what the bird is saying!

1	**A**	alert	**B**	familiar	**C**	aware	**D**	sensitive
2	**A**	origin	**B**	source	**C**	point	**D**	base
3	**A**	notice	**B**	catch	**C**	realise	**D**	tell
4	**A**	reply	**B**	behave	**C**	respond	**D**	act
5	**A**	Believe	**B**	Presume	**C**	Consider	**D**	Imagine
6	**A**	method	**B**	nature	**C**	manner	**D**	process
7	**A**	threat	**B**	risk	**C**	danger	**D**	fear
8	**A**	look	**B**	figure	**C**	watch	**D**	carry

Part 2

For questions **9–16**, read the text below and think of the word which best fits each gap. Use only **one** word in each gap. There is an example at the beginning **(0)**.

Write your answers **IN CAPITAL LETTERS on the separate answer sheet**.

Example:

0	Y	O	U																

How I met a good friend

Can **(0)** .... still remember the first time you met your best friend? I can clearly recall meeting mine – Jennifer. It was just after I'd started at a new school. On my first day, I'd **(9)** .... friends with a really nice girl whose name was Karin, and the following day, I decided to invite her to my house after school. I waited in the playground that morning **(10)** .... that I could speak to her. The ridiculous thing **(11)** .... though, that looking at the crowds of girls heading into the school, I suddenly realised I couldn't remember **(12)** .... of them was Karin! I simply didn't recognise her **(13)** .... all. In the end I just invited another girl that I'd also got on **(14)** .... quite well – and that was Jennifer.

However, I could never **(15)** .... imagined back then that, years later, Jennifer would still be **(16)** .... of my closest friends. For that reason, I'm quite grateful that I didn't manage to find Karin on that day years ago!

Part 3

For questions **17–24**, read the text below. Use the word given in capitals at the end of some of the lines to form a word that fits in the gap **in the same line**. There is an example at the beginning **(0)**.

Write your answers **IN CAPITAL LETTERS on the separate answer sheet.**

Example:

0	P	O	P	U	L	A	R	I	T	Y								

Pizza

Pizza is a food that enjoys **(0)** .... world-wide. It has a long **POPULAR**

history. Pizza as we know it today came into **(17)** .... in the **EXIST**

city of Naples in the 1700s.

Naples was by then becoming a major **(18)** .... city and **INDUSTRY**

large numbers of people were moving there for work. Many of the city's

(19) .... were poor. They wanted food that was nourishing **INHABIT**

but **(20)** .... Pizza could be made with cheap, simple and **EXPENSE**

(21) .... available ingredients, and so was ideal. **READY**

The **(22)** .... of tomatoes into Italian cuisine in the 18th and **INTRODUCE**

early 19th centuries finally gave us the true modern Italian pizza. Even

though tomatoes had reached Italy by the 1530s, it was widely thought

that they were a **(23)** .... fruit and, therefore, were only grown **POISON**

for decoration.

Pizza gradually spread to other parts of Italy and when the first pizzeria

opened in the USA in 1905, it started to become the **(24)** .... **INTERNATIONAL**

known and loved dish it is today.

Part 4

For questions **25–30**, complete the second sentence so that it has a similar meaning to the first sentence, using the word given. **Do not change the word given**. You must use between **two** and **five** words, including the word given. Here is an example **(0)**.

Example:

0   Prizes are given out when the school year finishes.

   PLACE

   Prize-giving .... end of the school year.

The gap can be filled by the words 'takes place at the', so you write:

Example:	**0**	*TAKES PLACE AT THE*

Write **only** the missing words **IN CAPITAL LETTERS on the separate answer sheet**.

---

25   Jack immediately raised his hand when the teacher asked if anyone had a question.

   HESITATE

   Jack .... up his hand when the teacher asked if anyone had a question.

26   You should get your mum's permission to come with us to the cinema.

   BETTER

   You .... for your mum's permission to come with us to the cinema.

27   Everyone gave in their homework apart from Charlie.

   EXCEPTION

   Everyone gave in their homework .... Charlie.

28 As Mum isn't home yet, I think it's possible that she missed her usual train.

MIGHT

As Mum isn't home yet, I think she .... caught her usual train.

29 I'm not really in the mood to go for a bike ride today.

LIKE

I don't really .... for a bike ride today.

30 Ben doesn't usually train hard enough to win any swimming races.

UNLESS

Ben won't win any swimming races .... than usual.

Part 5

You are going to read an article about a long-distance motor race called the Dakar Rally. For questions **31–36**, choose the answer (**A**, **B**, **C** or **D**) which you think fits best according to the text.

Mark your answers on the separate answer sheet.

My ambition: taking part in the Dakar Rally

By Amber Watts, 15 years old

Motorsports are my passion, and one day I'd love to challenge myself by taking part in the Dakar Rally. The rally is a long-distance off-road race, which runs for 15 days across varied terrain, with drivers having to cope with desert, mud and rocks. So tough is definitely the word you'd use to describe it. I think that's what appeals to me so much about it. Dad and I follow the race every year on TV, so I've got quite a good knowledge of it now. We're really into engineering and adapting vehicles – Dad's got this old jeep that we've been working on, making it suitable for tricky off-road driving.

In the Dakar Rally, you can drive any vehicle – motorbike, two- or four-wheel drives, even trucks! They're heavily adapted, so you need a lot of experience as a mechanic. They have to
line 19 be modified in order to be able to withstand the journey – you couldn't do it in an ordinary car because it would just fall apart! You don't need to be a professional rally driver to take part, but it helps having experience driving in difficult conditions. As well as all of that, it's a case of saving up a lot of money because the whole thing is *really* expensive, from investing in spare parts for the vehicle, to buying a two-week supply of fuel and other supplies.

I first became interested in the rally after being lucky enough to catch the launch of the race one year when I was on holiday. There was a definite tension in the air the day before the race. From where we were standing we could see the area where the teams – drivers and their mechanics – were making repairs and preparations which could only be done at the last minute. All I could see was a mechanic's legs sticking out from under each vehicle and everyone getting on quietly with the task at hand, helping each other out, despite the pressure.

Next day, we headed down to the starting line. I'd expected the vehicles to set off all at once, and when they left one by one, I really didn't know what was going on. Then I overheard someone saying that it was what's known as a time trial. Every vehicle, whether it's a motorbike or a lorry, is timed, and the fastest to complete the route is the winner in each category. Off they went in turn, in a cloud of dust and their engines revving at an incredible volume. I'd never seen anything like it and, before I knew it, the cars had disappeared from sight.

That experience encouraged me to find out more about this amazing race. The route is around 10,000 kilometres long, depending on which country it takes place in, so there's a lot of driving involved. You mustn't lose concentration for a minute and that's what really puts the drivers to the test. You also can't possibly imagine what you're going to encounter ahead – meeting obstacles, skidding on loose stones, crossing rivers, breaking down, you name it. It must be exhausting and thrilling at the same time. But you can't just go full speed ahead like you would on a race-track or you'd tire yourself out on the first day and it'd be really hard to keep going.

The competitors are given a map and have to find their way themselves. Comprehensive instructions are included on this map; however, given the fact that there are few landmarks along the way, this must be really demanding when you're unfamiliar with the territory. Some people get lost, and end up in the wrong place, but they just have to find their way back to the route again. Each day, the drivers aim to complete a particular stage. If they encounter setbacks which mean they don't make it, they spend an uncomfortable night with whatever hazards that might involve. Finishing the race is, therefore, a major achievement.

31 Amber is attracted to the idea of participating in the Dakar Rally because she

    A enjoys taking part in motorsports events.
    B likes the idea of doing something so difficult.
    C has been involved in preparing a vehicle for it.
    D has learned a lot about it from her father.

32 What does 'able to withstand' in line 19 mean?

    A economical enough to run throughout
    B strong enough to endure
    C large enough to cope with
    D advanced enough to be successful at

33 What made an impression on Amber when she saw teams preparing for a race?

    A how late some of them had left it
    B how excited everyone seemed to be
    C how well they were working together
    D how many people were involved

34 How does Amber say she felt as she stood at the starting line?

    A grateful to another spectator
    B concerned by the noise
    C interested to learn about the vehicles
    D surprised at what happened

35 In the fifth paragraph, what does Amber say is especially challenging about driving?

    A coping with its effects on the body
    B staying focused for long periods of time
    C being able to keep up the required pace
    D trying to predict what is coming next

36 What does Amber say about the guidance drivers are given?

    A It provides a high level of detail.
    B It can be interpreted in different ways.
    C It is straightforward to follow.
    D It highlights possible dangers.

Part 6

You are going to read an article about the discovery of new species of penguins. Six sentences have been removed from the article. Choose from the sentences **A–G** the one which fits each gap (**37–42**). There is one extra sentence which you do not need to use.

Mark your answers on the separate answer sheet.

The discovery of three new species of penguins

When you think of scientists discovering new species, you probably imagine them searching the Amazon rainforest or the depths of the oceans. However, these days, most new species are discovered by comparing genes in a science laboratory. New species can look so similar to their relatives that it is only the study of their DNA that reveals their differences.

Thanks to the abundance of genetic data that's now available, we're in the middle of a second era of biodiversity discovery. **37** And now, penguins can be added too. Following analysis of what was thought to be one species of penguin called the gentoo, it's become clear that it's not one single species at all.

In their study of gentoo penguins, scientists analysed genetic differences among colonies of gentoo across the Southern Ocean, including groups from the Falkland Islands (*Islas Malvinas*), South Georgia Island, the Antarctic Peninsula and Kerguelen Island. They discovered that gentoo penguins from these various regions don't interbreed. **38** King penguins, for example, are known to breed between colonies, even when separated by as much as 7,500km of ocean.

At first glance, the four groups of gentoo penguins appear very alike. **39** In fact, the physical and genetic distinctions are sufficient for the gentoo penguin to have been reclassified as four penguin species: *P. papua* from the Falkland Islands, *P. ellsworthi* from Antarctica, *P. poncetii* from South Georgia, and *P. taeniata* from Kerguelen Island.

The four species live in distinct environmental conditions across a large range of latitudes. *P. ellsworthi*, for example, is found on the cold, icy Antarctic Peninsula. This contrasts with the milder conditions experienced by *P. taeniata*, which lives much further from the South Pole. **40** The more southerly species eat more krill – small, shrimp-like crustaceans – and fewer fish. Scientists say that they now need to understand how the four gentoo species have each adapted to their conditions and how they are likely to respond to future environmental changes.

The division of gentoo penguins also has important implications for conservation. Gentoo penguins have been categorised as 'of least concern' on the international list of endangered species. **41** However, the increase was recorded before the discovery of the four separate gentoo species. In fact, of these four reclassified species only *P. ellsworthi* was found to be thriving. The conservation status of the other three species remains unclear, but given their location on isolated islands far north of the Antarctic Peninsula, they're almost certainly being affected by climate change. Consequently, the conservation status of all four species will need to be urgently assessed.

42 However, the discovery of the four new species highlights how little we still understand about the amazing diversity of life around us. That's why scientists say it's clear that we must continue to seek out new species. This is our best chance of preserving biodiversity. Without such efforts, we face losing species that we never even knew existed.

A	This was unexpected, because it contrasted sharply with the behaviour of other species.	**E**	Penguins are among the best-loved and most easily-recognised creatures on Earth.
B	And it's not just their habitat which is different.	**F**	In the past ten years, scientists have identified new species of giraffes, dolphins, birds and orangutans.
C	It therefore brings the total number of penguin species to twenty-one.	**G**	This is because the total number of these penguins has risen over the past decade.
D	When their skulls, beaks and legs are measured, though, significant differences become clear.		

Part 7

You are going to read an article about teenage writers and their favourite books. For questions **43–52**, choose from the writers (**A–D**). The writers may be chosen more than once.

Mark your answers on the separate answer sheet.

Which writer says that their favourite book

clearly benefitted their own creative work?

| 43 | |

made them look at a particular academic subject in a new way?

| 44 | |

revealed the limitations of one of their interests?

| 45 | |

completely transformed their reading preferences?

| 46 | |

encouraged them to try reading books of the same genre?

| 47 | |

influenced their view on the importance of reading widely?

| 48 | |

is rarely included in any recommendations they make about reading?

| 49 | |

inspired them to start producing their own fiction?

| 50 | |

wouldn't have featured in their reading if they hadn't been obliged to study it?

| 51 | |

exceeded the expectations they had when they first came across it?

| 52 | |

My favourite book

Four teenage writers talk about the book they've most enjoyed reading.

A Tomasz

I discovered my favourite book *Mind Games* by Ursula Waters in a second-hand bookshop. It was obviously sci-fi – something I'm not usually a fan of and didn't really think I'd appreciate much – but it had an unusual-looking cover which made me decide to buy it. Anyway, I started reading and instantly took to it. The author's sense of wonder that came through was a real surprise, and I loved how she made everything seem interesting and mysterious at the same time. As a result, and alongside my usual novels, I began to explore a few other sci-fi writers' work. And the stuff I read had a profound effect on my fiction writing, which I was just beginning to get into. I definitely owe a great debt of gratitude to Ursula Waters.

B Ana

My favourite book is *Points to Consider* by John Meadows, although having said that, I'd be the first to admit that it's far too long and quite complex – not that that would normally put me off. But it was required reading for a philosophy assignment I needed to do – otherwise I'd never have bothered picking it up, to be honest. And even now, if people ask me for ideas about something good to read, I hardly ever mention it. On the other hand, it was the first book I'd read on philosophy that provided me with fresh insights into the topic. For this reason, I've returned to the book many times and I'd say it's really changed how I think about things. Actually that's influenced my choice of degree course at university – and it'll probably affect the writing I'm doing.

C Jack

A Life by James Melville was a book I'd never even heard of before I read it but it absolutely knocked me out. It's all about his own life and in it he discusses the books that shaped him as a writer. I found it astonishing and it totally changed what I chose to read afterwards. Reading his book made it clear he knew a huge amount about different areas of study – languages, history, you name it. And as an aspiring writer myself, I realised after reading his book that it was essential for authors to be extremely well-read before they ever start to create anything themselves. Melville hadn't limited himself to reading the works of well-known writers, either, which was one reason why I avoided bestsellers. In comparison with other stuff I was reading, and especially what I'd been introduced to through Melville, they seemed really shallow.

D Sally

I've loved books ever since I learned to read, and one thing I've discovered is that the surest way to learn is to tackle stuff that really gets your brain working. It might be tough, but it's worth it. And that was never more true than with my favourite book, a lengthy novel called *Techno* by Nat Jones. Thanks to this book, I became aware that my obsession with technology was never going to help me achieve many of the things I wanted out of life. The author's views, cleverly expressed through the main character, were all about what technology can and can't do, and if I hadn't read it, I'd probably have ended up working in software development or something. Instead, reading this has encouraged me to become a short story writer, which suits my personality much better, even though I haven't had much success so far.

WRITING (1 hour 20 minutes)

Part 1

You **must** answer this question. Write your answer in **140–190** words in an appropriate style on the separate answer sheet.

1   In your English class you have been talking about making choices. Now your English teacher has asked you to write an essay.

Write your essay using **all** the notes and giving reasons for your point of view.

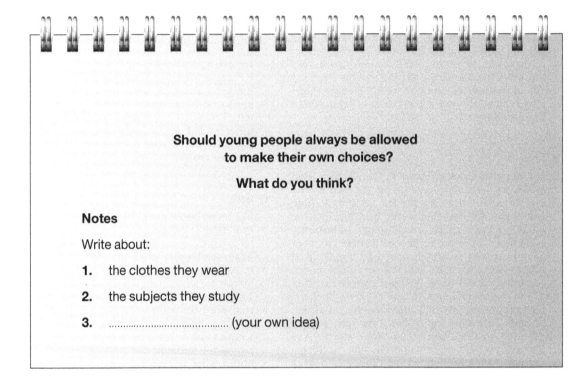

**Should young people always be allowed
to make their own choices?**

What do you think?

Notes

Write about:

1.   the clothes they wear

2.   the subjects they study

3.   .... (your own idea)

Part 2

Write an answer to **one** of the questions **2–4** in this part. Write your answer in **140–190** words in an appropriate style on the separate answer sheet. Put the question number in the box at the top of the answer sheet.

---

2 You see this announcement on an English-language website.

> **Articles wanted**
>
> ## Going to Mars
>
> Many scientists and astronauts are making plans to visit the planet Mars, a journey that could take eight months. If you had the opportunity to join them, would you go?
>
> What do you think might be difficult about the trip?
>
> *The best articles will be posted on our website.*

Write your **article**.

3 This is an email you have received from an English-speaking friend, Sam.

> Hi
>
> My parents think I spend too much time playing computer games. They want me to find a new hobby that will get me out of the house. What do you think I should do?
>
> Sam

Write your **email**.

4 You see this announcement on an English-language website.

> **Reviews wanted**
>
> ## A shopping centre
>
> Is there a shopping centre in your area? If so, write us a review of it!
>
> Tell us what you think is good for teenagers about the shopping centre, and what you feel could be improved there.
>
> *The best reviews will be posted on our website.*

Write your **review**.

LISTENING (approximately 40 minutes)

Part 1

You will hear people talking in eight different situations.
For questions **1–8**, choose the best answer (**A**, **B** or **C**).

Listening test audio

---

1   You hear a girl talking about a television studio she visited on a school trip.

What surprised her?

A   how unfriendly the people were

B   how untidy the sets were

C   how crowded the building was

2   You hear a girl talking to her father about her career plans.

What does he recommend?

A   finding out about a range of opportunities

B   improving some of the skills she would need

C   getting work experience in the school holidays

3   You hear a boy telling a friend about his new phone.

How is he feeling?

A   disappointed with its appearance

B   frustrated by a repeated problem

C   confused about how to set it up

4   You hear two friends talking about a game called Sokatira.

What do they both say about the game?

A   It was more interesting than other games they know.

B   It was physically difficult to play.

C   It was challenging to remember the rules.

5 You hear two friends talking about something called the Paleo diet.

What does the boy think about it?

A It is probably based on a mistaken belief.

B It is a shame that it may not be very healthy.

C It is something that would be beneficial for him.

6 You hear two friends talking about a pop concert.

They both think that

A the tickets aren't value for money.

B some of the bands aren't very good.

C the venue isn't particularly convenient.

7 You hear two friends talking about a TV series.

What do they agree about the reviews of the series?

A They were influenced by the director's previous work.

B They over-emphasised one specific weakness.

C They failed to understand its intention.

8 You hear a girl telling a friend about a favour she's doing for her grandfather.

She regrets not

A remembering where she put something.

B listening more carefully to instructions.

C having enough time to complete a task properly.

Part 2

You will hear a teenager called Ben giving a presentation about his interest in bats. For questions **9–18**, complete the sentences with a word or short phrase.

Listening test audio

Bats

Ben says there are **(9)** .... species of bats worldwide.

Ben says some people wrongly believe that the diet of UK bats includes

(10) ....

Ben admits that, at one time, he thought bats were **(11)** ....

Seeing lots of bats in a **(12)** .... is when
Ben initially became interested in them.

Ben describes the species called the Greater Horseshoe Bat as being the size of a

(13) ....

Ben helped to make a **(14)** .... near his school in order to attract bats.

A competition to create **(15)** .... was
particularly popular among Ben's schoolmates.

Ben produced a **(16)** .... for people
going on a 'bat walk' around his local area.

Ben says **(17)** .... are the main
reason why bats stay away from people's gardens.

Ben says he would like to do research into how bats

(18) .... when he's older.

Part 3

You will hear five short extracts in which teenagers are talking about a transport survey they did in town as part of a school project. For questions **19–23**, choose from the list (**A–H**) what the speaker says about the activity. Use the letters only once. There are three extra letters which you do not need to use.

Listening test audio

A I was unsure how to record the data.

B Some of the information we collected surprised me.

| | Speaker 1 | | 19 |

C I enjoyed the change to the normal school routine.

| | Speaker 2 | | 20 |

D I felt embarrassed surveying people I didn't know.

| | Speaker 3 | | 21 |

E My feelings about the activity changed as I did it.

| | Speaker 4 | | 22 |

F My group ran out of time before completing the task.

| | Speaker 5 | | 23 |

G At first I misunderstood the instructions.

H I was pleased to be given a particular role in the group.

Part 4

You will hear teenage cyclist Joe Anderson talking about his racing career in cycling so far. For questions **24–30**, choose the best answer (**A**, **B** or **C**).

Listening test audio

24   What does Joe say about choosing cycling as his main sport?

    A He was determined to do something he really enjoyed.

    B He was responding to pressure from his family.

    C He was upset by his lack of ability in other events.

25   How did Joe feel after taking part in his first major cycling race?

    A motivated to continue in the sport

    B embarrassed about his performance

    C irritated by the attitude of other competitors

26   When talking about doing different kinds of cycling races, Joe reveals

    A the pleasure he gets from the variety.

    B a desire to experience new challenges.

    C his preference for individual events.

27   What was Joe's opinion of the summer camp he went on?

    A The experience was rather discouraging.

    B It was only useful for certain people.

    C Some activities provided were too easy.

28   Joe thinks that a particular problem he faced

    A caused him a great deal of stress.

    B showed him how to win races.

    C made him change his training strategy.

29 What's Joe's attitude towards certain activities of his training programme?

    A He resents the time some of them take.

    B He struggles to understand the advantage of them.

    C He dislikes the regular schedule he follows.

30 Joe thinks that his priorities now should include

    A setting aside time to spend with friends.

    B listening to advice from other people.

    C avoiding anything that might distract him.

35159

CAMBRIDGE
English

		Candidate Number	
Candidate Name			
Centre Name		Centre Number	
Examination Title		Examination Details	
Candidate Signature		Assessment Date	

Supervisor: If the candidate is ABSENT or has WITHDRAWN shade here ○

First for Schools Reading and Use of English Candidate Answer Sheet

Instructions
Use a PENCIL (B or HB).
Rub out any answer you want to change using an eraser.

Parts 1, 5, 6 and 7:
Mark ONE letter for each question.

For example, if you think A is the right answer to the question, mark your answer sheet like this:

Parts 2, 3 and 4: Write your answer clearly in CAPITAL LETTERS.

For parts 2 and 3, write one letter in each box. `0 EXAMPLE`

Part 1

	A	B	C	D
1	○	○	○	○
2	○	○	○	○
3	○	○	○	○
4	○	○	○	○
5	○	○	○	○
6	○	○	○	○
7	○	○	○	○
8	○	○	○	○

Part 2

		Do not write below here
9		9 1 0 ○ ○
10		10 1 0 ○ ○
11		11 1 0 ○ ○
12		12 1 0 ○ ○
13		13 1 0 ○ ○
14		14 1 0 ○ ○
15		15 1 0 ○ ○
16		16 1 0 ○ ○

Continues over ➡

35159

35159

Part 3

Do not write below here

#		1	0
17		○	○
18		○	○
19		○	○
20		○	○
21		○	○
22		○	○
23		○	○
24		○	○

Part 4

Do not write below here

#		2	1	0
25		○	○	○
26		○	○	○
27		○	○	○
28		○	○	○
29		○	○	○
30		○	○	○

Part 5

	A	B	C	D
31	○	○	○	○
32	○	○	○	○
33	○	○	○	○
34	○	○	○	○
35	○	○	○	○
36	○	○	○	○

Part 6

	A	B	C	D	E	F	G
37	○	○	○	○	○	○	○
38	○	○	○	○	○	○	○
39	○	○	○	○	○	○	○
40	○	○	○	○	○	○	○
41	○	○	○	○	○	○	○
42	○	○	○	○	○	○	○

Part 7

	A	B	C	D	E	F
43	○	○	○	○	○	○
44	○	○	○	○	○	○
45	○	○	○	○	○	○
46	○	○	○	○	○	○
47	○	○	○	○	○	○
48	○	○	○	○	○	○
49	○	○	○	○	○	○
50	○	○	○	○	○	○
51	○	○	○	○	○	○
52	○	○	○	○	○	○

35159

Sample answer sheet: Listening

CAMBRIDGE
English

Candidate Name	
Centre Name	
Examination Title	
Candidate Signature	

Candidate Number	
Centre Number	
Examination Details	
Assessment Date	

Supervisor: If the candidate is ABSENT or has WITHDRAWN shade here ○

First for Schools Listening Candidate Answer Sheet

Instructions
Use a PENCIL (B or HB).
Rub out any answer you want to change using an eraser.

Parts 1, 3 and **4:**
Mark ONE letter for each question.

For example, if you think **A** is the right answer to the question, mark your answer sheet like this:

`0` A B C

Part 2:
Write your answer clearly in CAPITAL LETTERS.

Write one letter or number in each box.
If the answer has more than one word, leave one box empty between words.

For example:

`0` N U M B E R 1 2

Turn this sheet over to start.

36863

Part 1

	A	B	C			A	B	C
1	○	○	○		5	○	○	○
2	○	○	○		6	○	○	○
3	○	○	○		7	○	○	○
4	○	○	○		8	○	○	○

Part 2 (Remember to write in CAPITAL LETTERS or numbers)

Do not write below here

9		9 1 0 ○ ○
10		10 1 0 ○ ○
11		11 1 0 ○ ○
12		12 1 0 ○ ○
13		13 1 0 ○ ○
14		14 1 0 ○ ○
15		15 1 0 ○ ○
16		16 1 0 ○ ○
17		17 1 0 ○ ○
18		18 1 0 ○ ○

Part 3

	A	B	C	D	E	F	G	H
19	○	○	○	○	○	○	○	○
20	○	○	○	○	○	○	○	○
21	○	○	○	○	○	○	○	○
22	○	○	○	○	○	○	○	○
23	○	○	○	○	○	○	○	○

Part 4

	A	B	C
24	○	○	○
25	○	○	○
26	○	○	○
27	○	○	○
28	○	○	○
29	○	○	○
30	○	○	○

36863

Part One Answer
You must write within the grey lines.

Part Two Answer
You must write within the grey lines.

Write your question number here:

Part Two Answer
You must write within the grey lines.

Write your question number here:	

SAMPLE

| **Part Two Answer** |
| You must write within the grey lines. |

Write your question number here: [ ]

(lined writing space, with "SAMPLE" watermark diagonally across the page)

Acknowledgements

The authors and publishers acknowledge the following sources of copyright material and are grateful for the permissions granted. While every effort has been made, it has not always been possible to identify the sources of all the material used, or to trace all copyright holders. If any omissions are brought to our notice, we will be happy to include the appropriate acknowledgements on reprinting and in the next update to the digital edition, as applicable.

Key: RUE = Reading and Use of English, S = Speaking, T = Test.

Text

RUE T1: The Guardian for the text adapted from 'Jamie Scott: the songwriting 'fixer' for everyone from Adele to Justin Bieber' by Eamonn Forde, *The Guardian*, 23.09.2016. Copyright © 2016 Guardian News & Media Limited. Reproduced with permission; Dogo News for the text adapted from 'Japans prestigious good design award goes to a world map', 11.01.2017. Copyright © 2017 Dogo News, Inc. Reproduced with permission; **RUE T2:** The Telegraph for the text adapted from 'Why humans cannot help fiddling with mobile phones at dinner' by Sarah Knapton, *The Telegraph,* 03.06.2016. Copyright © 2016 Telegraph Media Group Limited. Reproduced with permission; Dogo News for the text adapted from 'Sweden's Icehotel is now open 365 days a year', 26.11.2016. Copyright © 2016 Dogo News, Inc. Reproduced with permission; Dogo News for the text adapted from 'Surprise your pet fish may be able to recognize you', 19.08.2016. Copyright © 2016 Dogo News, Inc. Reproduced with permission; Orca Book Publishers for the text adapted from 'Snowboarders', by Jeff Ross, *The Drop*. Copyright © 2011 Orca Book Publishers. Reproduced with permission; New Scientist Ltd. for the text adapted from 'Plunging deep beneath the sea in a tiny sub to map the ocean' by Aviva Rutkin, *New Scientist*, 17.08.2016. Copyright © 2016 New Scientist Ltd. All rights reserved. Distributed by Tribune Content Agency. Reproduced with permission; **RUE T3:** The Guardian for the text adapted from 'The rise and rise of tabletop gaming' by Dan Jolin, *The Guardian*, 25.09.2016. Copyright © 2016 Guardian News & Media Limited. Reproduced with permission; Dogo News for the text adapted from 'Researchers stumble upon a treasure trove of ancient shipwrecks in the black sea', 14.11.2016. Copyright © 2016 Dogo News, Inc. Reproduced with permission; The Guardian for the text adapted from 'My workout: Stephanie Roberts, 23, flat water kayaker – "The water is a special place to be"' by Daniel Masoliver, *The Guardian*, 29.10.2016. Copyright © 2016 Guardian News & Media Limited. Reproduced with permission; The Guardian for the text adapted from 'My workout: 'Towards the end of a race, your legs are on fire' by Daniel Masoliver, *The Guardian*, 10.12.2016. Copyright © 2016 Guardian News & Media Limited. Reproduced with permission; The Guardian for the text adapted from 'My workout: Gary Clay, 55, surfer – 'Age is not an issue' by Daniel Masoliver, *The Guardian*, 20.08.2016. Copyright © 2016 Guardian News & Media Limited. Reproduced with permission; The Guardian for the text adapted from 'My workout: Amy Horton, 26, rock climber – 'It can be scary' by Daniel Masoliver, *The Guardian*, 10.09.2016. Copyright © 2016 Guardian News & Media Limited. Reproduced with permission; **RUE T4:** Jane Younger for the text adapted from 'How we discovered three new species of penguin in the Southern Ocean' by Jane Younger, The Conversation, 17.08.2016. Copyright © 2016 Jane Younger. Reproduced with kind permission.

Photography

All the photographs are sourced from Getty Images.

ST1: vgajic/E+; Jose Luis Pelaez Inc/DigitalVision; xavierarnau/E+; Carol Yepes/Moment; **ST2:** kali9/E+; David Madison/Stone; Lorado/E+; Sam Mellish/In Pictures; **ST3:** Jacobs Stock Photography Ltd/DigitalVision; Matthias Tunger/DigitalVision; Christopher Hopefitch/The Image Bank; Klaus Vedfelt/DigitalVision; **ST4:** SolStock/E+; NurPhoto; BFC/Ascent Xmedia/Photodisc; Chanin Wardkhian/Moment.

Audio

Audio production by dsound recording Ltd.

Typesetting

Typesetting by QBS Learning.

Visual materials for the Speaking test

Why are the people playing music in these situations?

1A

1B

Why have the people decided to study in these places?

1C

1D

1E

enjoying time
with friends

buying things
that they
don't need

**Is going shopping a good
way for young people to
spend their free time?**

the
advantages
of shopping
online

keeping up
to date with
fashion

having less
time for other
things

What is interesting for the students about the school trips?

2A

2B

Why are the teenagers doing these different sports?

2C

2D

2E

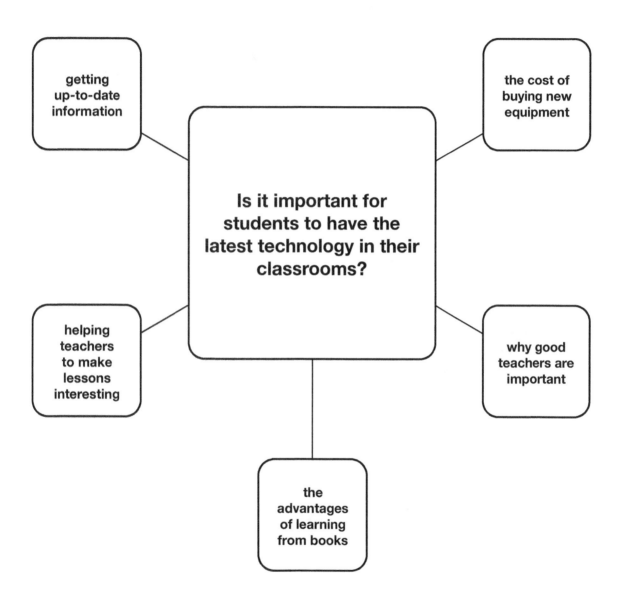

getting
up-to-date
information

the cost of
buying new
equipment

**Is it important for
students to have the
latest technology in their
classrooms?**

helping
teachers
to make
lessons
interesting

why good
teachers are
important

the
advantages
of learning
from books

Why might it be difficult for the people to decide what to buy in these situations?

3A

3B

Why do the people need help in these situations?

3C

3D

3E

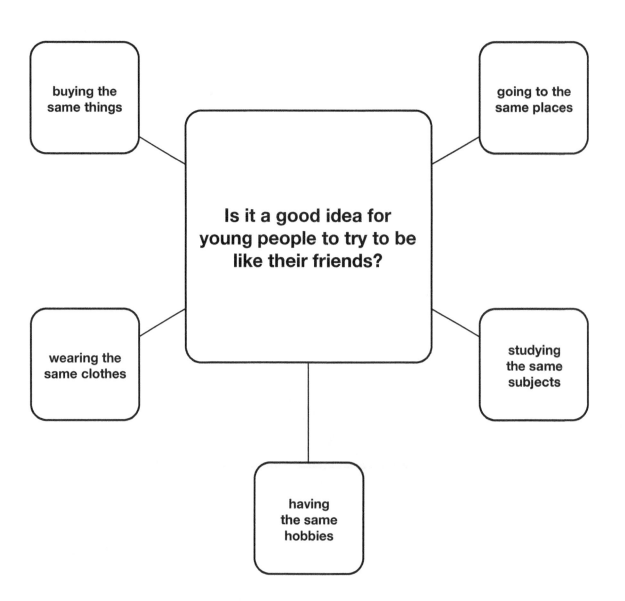

buying the
same things

going to the
same places

Is it a good idea for
young people to try to be
like their friends?

wearing the
same clothes

studying
the same
subjects

having
the same
hobbies

Why are the people running in these situations?

4A

4B

Why are the people explaining things in these situations?

4C

4D

4E

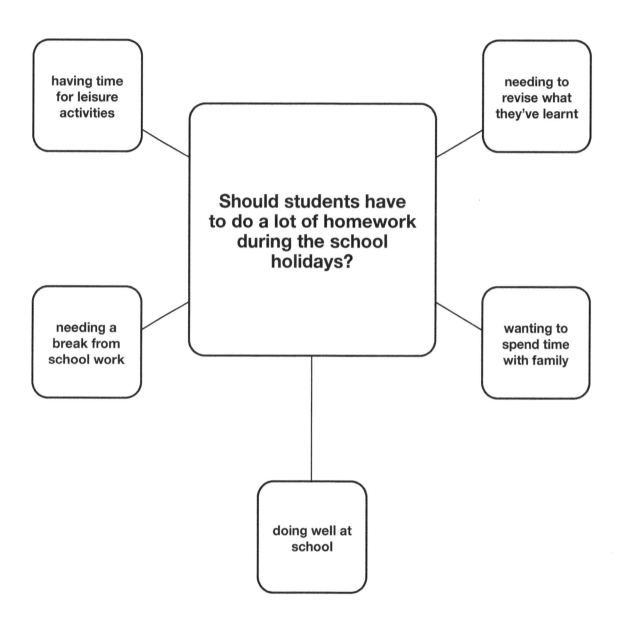

having time for leisure activities

needing to revise what they've learnt

Should students have to do a lot of homework during the school holidays?

needing a break from school work

wanting to spend time with family

doing well at school

Caiaimage/Sam Edwards/Getty

SPOT THE DIFFERENCE

That's right – there is no difference.

All our authentic practice tests go through the same design process as the official exam. We check every single part of our practice tests with real students under exam conditions, to make sure we give you the most authentic experience possible.

The official practice tests from Cambridge.